◄ a memoir ►

# Maditude

Misadventures of an angry young man

Paul Starsoneck

Copyright © 2014 Paul Starsoneck
All rights reserved.

ISBN-10: 099039140X
ISBN-13: 978-0-9903914-0-1

Cover Design by Jan Jewett, JKJ Design

First Edition

To Aunt Mae

# Contents

# Preface

If there's a secret club only for people who write
memoirs, I won't see an invitation. I'm not famous and I have
not overcome some great obstacle to succeed in life. In fact,
there was a time when people doubted if I had ever read a
book, never mind written one. What I have always been
blessed with is a very, very good memory. I remember not only
the events and people I observed, but also how I felt about
them at the time. Yes, as a youngster I could name all the State
Capitols and the U.S. Presidents, but instead of studying the
periodic table next, I chose to memorize the college attended
by every player in the National Basketball Association in 1974.
When I wasn't reading *Basketball Digest*, I used my ability to
recall information to get good grades in school without
studying, to test well, and to achieve success in a business
career for nearly thirty years. I've also had a great deal of good
fortune and it's time to recognize it.

Why should you read this book? Because when I remember the events and thinking of my youth, it reflects the process all kids go through in finding their way in the world. You'll see that the lessons kids discover are tied to the perspective they bring. You'll read stories about how I learned what to do by learning what not to do. Like riding on the wrong side of the road, or swearing at your grade school teacher or a nun. Then there are stories about how I discovered who I am by first finding out who I was not: not gifted, not a natural athlete, not a fisherman, not a townie. Finally, you'll be introduced to a series of people who helped me along the way. How they did may inspire you to try to do the same for a young person in your life.

. . . . .

It's my fifth birthday and kids from school and the neighborhood are gathered at our house for a party. It's rare that friends are at our house and I anticipate this to be the grand social event of the spring season of 1967. Kids are sitting around the kitchen table waiting for the cake to be cut and the games like Pin the Tail on the Donkey to resume, but there's one problem. The birthday boy is missing. He's under the table; sitting with arms folded across his bent knees, scowl on his face. That's me and I can't possibly imagine why these other kids are winning games and prizes at MY birthday party. I should win all the prizes and get all the gifts. They can have cake and ice cream, but that's it. Left up to me, I would order everyone out of the house, right now!

I was a hotheaded, selfish, foul-mouthed kid. When I got angry with someone or something, I stayed mad. I had bouts of this before I was old enough to realize it. The reoccurrence of this is best described as "Maditude." Maditude is listed in the *Urban Dictionary* as:

While attitude is a settled way of thinking or feeling, typically reflected in a person's behavior. Maditude is an extreme, nearly delusional case of attitude. When someone's bad attitude radiates off of them, putting everyone else in the same Maditude.

My story is about discovering this definition and its impact. It's a wobbly ride on the banana seat of my bicycle, or a jarring pothole run over in my Jeep Renegade. Hopefully, you will see yourselves or your children in these encounters and laugh at how a young mind, lacking perspective, struggles to make choices. How someone looking for understanding of how the world works may be looking in the wrong places, paying careful attention to the wrong things.

I think we all get mad and we are all capable of developing a bad attitude. But if you let it encompass your entire outlook and interaction with the world, you'll find things won't go your way, despite your best efforts. Your biggest obstacle is the effect you have on other people and you don't realize it because you can't see through your own cloud of anger.

When you hear people say, "You can't tell that kid anything, he knows everything," they meant me. Even if the perfect parents had raised me, I wouldn't have listened to their advice. I believe in personal responsibility, you own who you become. I have read many biographies and memoirs of people who overcame great difficulties of circumstances and events. This is not one of those stories. This is a story about overcoming yourself. Of how to develop an understanding of people and how to relate to the world. Understanding how your actions and your attitude influence how people treat you, not vice versa. Knowing a lot, and thinking that you know everything, can actually mean you know very little about life. My Maditude is well under control, but not completely gone.

People who know me well today can argue about just how far it is below the surface.

.  .  .  .  .

On any given Saturday we would stop by my grandmother's house on Mauran Avenue in East Providence, Rhode Island. My Aunt Mae would be running the family control center, as various siblings would be coming and going, often with their children in tow, my cousins. My grandmother would always be sitting in the same cushioned rocking chair in the kitchen, arguing in Portuguese. She would often object to something I was doing, but my Aunt Mae would argue back in my favor. I spoke no Portuguese, so I only knew it was an argument by the volume, tone, and occasional translation by Aunt Mae. I would retreat from the kitchen to the small parlor that overlooked the front porch to find my grumpy Uncle Willie in the armchair with his stinky feet. He never spoke to me directly and seemed to be in a constant state of irritation. He was an anti-social bachelor and lived his entire life in that house, as far as I knew. I would hope for a game to be on the television and Aunt Mae's husband Jesse to be in there watching it. He was always kind and we shared a love for our local baseball team, the Boston Red Sox.

Uncle Johnny might stop in. He was friendly and smiling but described by his siblings as "never the same since the war," his service in World War II. His emotional problems became more evident as he grew older, leading to estrangement and heartache. I might find boisterous Uncle Tony sitting at the kitchen table drinking coffee, laughing and telling stories. My mother Alice would say Tony was a B.S. artist, but I liked him because he seemed to be having fun. I guess the stories were a little longer and louder with his drinking buddies at the Knights of Columbus. When I was thirteen he bought me a beer in the bar during a cousin's wedding, while we watched the Red Sox and Luis Tiant shut out the three time defending champion Oakland A's in the '75 playoffs.

All of my mother's siblings lived in small houses close to my grandparents. Johnny and Tony resided in adjacent backyards. Mae, and the youngest son Danny, lived a couple of miles away. Alice, the one who moved away, was just six miles down the road in Riverside. Uncle Danny was always friendly and well liked by my sister Karen and me. He had two girls our ages and the two families would get together off and on at the beach or campground. Danny also had a nervous personality that came most frequently to the forefront in argumentative exchanges with Alice.

Not only did the clan settle in close proximity, but also they didn't travel far either. They worked, attended Mass, and had social interactions in the close radius of home. They had a cautious, almost foreboding view of the larger world outside their familiar confines. It may have been part of their shared experience as immigrants, or something common in their genome, but it didn't resonate in me. They had come from San Miguel in the Azores, a chain of islands off Portugal. I imagined the spirits of the great Portuguese explorers like Vasco da Gama, Balboa, and Cabral, prompting their voyage to the New World, but in reality I'm sure they came for the same reasons as many immigrants, a chance for a better life. Now any exploration seemed to begin and end in East Providence. Maybe the explorer's gene had skipped a generation, as I was determined early on to do the opposite of whatever anyone told me. I was going to try new places and things, and overcome any instincts of caution.

"Your mother was very sick when you were young." I heard this said several times from my relatives with scant details accompanying it. She was bedridden, she had pneumonia, and she had a nervous breakdown. These were all things she would also say, but did they all happen together? Was it post-partum depression when I arrived? I did come to realize she suffered ongoing bouts with anxiety and depression, but I was too young to understand this during my formative years. Later in life Alice sought and received help with these issues, and with modern medication lives a happier and healthier life. It's not uncommon to be hear her say:

"If I only had this medication when I was younger I would have had a very different life."

It's fair to say we might all have had a very different life. But this story is not about that. These are my memories of an often-misguided kid and how he learned to co-exist, and then thrive in the world around him.

# "Awful, Awful"

In the middle of a hot and humid summer Stephen and I had the idea to ride our bikes 10 miles to the Newport Creamery in Barrington. My mother, Alice, of course had forbidden it, this time due to the humidity. We would ride the five miles out to the creamery and drink up our favorite extra thick milk shakes, the "Awful, Awful." Coffee was the preferred flavor. So that day Stephen and I set out towards our summer refreshment, but with a slight change. Stephen was riding his older brother Ricky's new fangled ten speed bike. No more banana seat and wide handle bars. While this may have been more efficient for a longer ride, it put Stephen in a prone riding position with his feet barely reaching the pedals.

The ride there was uneventful as we climbed the hill on Maple Avenue in the bucolic suburban setting of Barrington. Traffic was light in the early afternoon as we reached the creamery parking lot and ordered our coffee milkshakes through the takeout window. The super dense shakes took some time to consume. The advertising campaign was a dare: "Drink Three, Get One Free." They had nothing to worry about that day, one was enough for us.

Satiated, we set out for our return trip in mid afternoon. We hadn't realized that traffic would be getting heavier at 3 or 3:30 p.m. on a summer afternoon in Barrington: kids being picked up from camp, the YMCA, or other organized summer activities that were a rarity in Riverside.

As we descended the Maple Avenue hill, we soon had a choice to make. Ride along the roadside or over on the sidewalk itself. As the hill grew steeper, the road narrowed and the sidewalk separated, ending on a three-foot grassy roadside embankment. We chose the road for its smoother surface, coasting downhill with the now shoulder high sidewalk on our left, facing traffic instead of riding with it on the right. As we approached the bottom of the hill, a steady stream of cars was making left turns to climb the hill. I started using my coaster brake when I saw our travel lane shrinking at the apex of the turning cars. As I did this I heard Stephen yell from behind, "Don't stop!"

He was having trouble getting enough leverage on the brake levers of the oversized ten-speed. I stopped braking and could feel him closing in from behind. Just as I reached the narrowest point of passage, the right grip of my wide handlebars began skidding along the front right quarter panel of an approaching car. This sent my front wheel sideways while throwing me off the bike. I tumbled along the grass embankment. Stephen was close behind, frantically trying to slow down as his travel path now included the stopped car and my downed bike. He clipped the front of the car and was thrown over the handlebars, skidding along the hood and eventually landing on the ground. We shook ourselves to our feet. Stephen came over to check on me:

"You all right?"

"Yeah, how 'bout you?"

"OK."

We sat on the sidewalk with our forearms pulling at our knees. The stunned woman driving the vehicle was coming over to check on us with a look of fright usually reserved for the Saturday afternoon "Creature Double Feature." Stephen turned to me and asked, "Is my lip cut?"

As he bared his teeth, I could see the problem. One front tooth was broken in half, the other completely gone from his bloody smile.

"Your tooth's gone!"

"Shit, help me look for it!"

We eventually found his tooth on the roadside with the help of the paramedics from the rescue squad and a firefighter from the truck. The driver of the car was shaken up and she had insisted on calling them, against our wishes. I had tears forming when they said Stephen had to ride to the hospital with them.

"What d'ya crying about? I'm the one who lost the tooth."

It wasn't the tooth, but the thought that I had caused the accident. Stephen took off with the siren blaring all the way to the hospital. He was checked out and quickly released to the custody of his disgusted and less than empathetic mother. She mostly fumed that he shouldn't have been riding Ricky's bike.

I had a wonderful ride home in a police cruiser with my mangled bike in the truck. It was now the end of the day and my father was home. While this may have been a bad break for most kids, it actually helped my cause in keeping Alice's

Paul Starsoneck

reaction a bit saner. My good fortune continued in a number of ways. The cop did not come to the door. I was able to shuttle my bike to the shed before any real inspection. I was able to frame the incident as Stephen having an accident with a car in Barrington. I had to deal with being late for dinner, having the police car come to the house, and ignoring my mother in taking the forbidden ride to Barrington due to the high humidity. This fed straight into my father's standard comment about his discomfort:

"It's not the heat, it's the humidity."

In the days following Stephen visited the dentist and was given a "partial," a metal plate with a false tooth that neatly fit into the gap in his smile. The recovered tooth was of no use. The second broken front tooth was capped. By the time school started up again, he had learned to wiggle his tongue against the plate causing the false tooth to drop in and out of its slot. He found this to be of great shock value with the fifth grade girls at Alice M. Waddington School. I managed to straighten my handlebars, remove a crumpled front fender and return my bike to working order without any further disclosure to my father.

18

The following fall Stephen and I tried out and made the St. Brendan's CYO (Catholic Youth Organization) basketball team with Stephen as a scrappy guard and myself as a less than fleet footed forward. My interest in basketball grew from the Saturday morning recreational league for eight and nine year olds at the Oldham Elementary School gym to CYO teams for a single reason: I was pretty good early on and even better if you only read the game recaps in the East Providence Post weekly newspaper. Alice saved some clippings regaling my "running one-hander" to win a playoff game. I was competitive as always and even got to see my Uncle Jesse, the school janitor, each Saturday morning during the season.

At St. Brendan's it was a different story. Try-outs were held in the church gym with Coach Don Paiva running us through a series of drills before grouping us into short scrimmages. Once on the squad, we practiced two hours on Tuesday and Thursday evenings and played a game each week on Sunday afternoons. Alice and Ed attended the home games and even traveled to the seven other parish gyms in the East Bay region. My participation seemed to represent some sort of status to Alice in terms of the church parishioners.

She was an adamant churchgoer, attending mass weekly and frequenting confession on Saturday afternoons. She insisted Karen and I do the same. Looking back I think we were better for it. Ed was from a Protestant household but not religious in any detectable way. He didn't attend mass and I didn't get the impression he cared much for the basketball games either. Our first year on the team was mainly on the bench as the twelve year olds dominated the playing time.

Being part of the team had some unexpected benefits. We traveled to some tournaments around the state, giving me a glimpse into other towns and facilities. We won the East Bay tournament and advanced to the state tournament, eventually finishing runner-up to Our Lady of Providence (OLP). This resulted in trophies and a green jacket stitched with East Bay Champions and St. Brendan's above the angry leprechaun mascot of the Fighting Irish. I wore that windbreaker jacket over a hooded sweatshirt every day until it disintegrated.

We hosted an annual Christmas tournament at St. Brendan's, which consisted of three other teams, invited from outside the East Bay league. This coincided with the Christmas bazaar and drew a surprisingly large crowd on a Saturday. During the first game between the two invitees, our team waited in the hall and stairwells connecting the gym to the rest of the Catholic school. Our cheerleaders joined us. Yes, we even had fully uniformed cheerleading parish girls.

The girls being more mature at similar ages introduced us to a way to pass the time until our game started. We sat cross-legged in a circle as one girl produced an empty soda bottle, which she spun on the ground, and then kissed the boy it pointed at. Wow, this basketball team stuff is great! I especially liked it when one of the girls forced the bottle to point at me and gave me my first kiss. Luckily this happened before an angry nun confiscated the bottle and broke up the circle, admonishing us all. For the next couple of weeks I walked around drinking bottled soda from vending machines hoping for a young girl to rush over to me.

I've always been conflicted in my feelings towards St. Brendan's. I obviously enjoyed the social aspects of CYO and many of the community-oriented activities like food drives, car washes, and paper drives for charitable causes. Some of our priests were very approachable, likeable, and focused on the community as a whole. Amongst the clergy and the lay people of the church there were some positive behavioral models that helped define good and bad, right and wrong for me. I did not at all appreciate the fire and brimstone manner of a few of our priests and the violent images they drew out of scripture to reinforce their points. If lines could be drawn that sharply between right and wrong, good and bad, then we were all hypocrites the moment we left mass. Towards the end of a typical Catholic mass there is a moment when parishioners turn to each other and say, "Peace be with you" while shaking hands. I was particularly troubled that Alice both wished her fellow congregants peace and for them to dress better. The wardrobe commentary would be offered before we left the parking lot along with admonishments of other drivers as we fought to beat them out of the lot.

. . . . .

An evening that stands out in life at 160 Holland Avenue occurred so early it may not have been remembered without the constant reminder of the hole in the linen closet door. I was young enough to be in the bathtub with my sister, who was four and a half years my senior. I can barely remember playing with plastic boats in the water. I guess we were told to get out of the bath and get ready for bed, but we continued playing in the tub for a while.

Alice reappeared with dramatic flair as she slammed the bathroom door open driving the knob through the linen closet door. She screamed hysterically. Her eyes were wide with rage. Karen and I leapt to our feet, but were unable to step out of the tub in fear of the wild animal now loose in the room. After another few minutes of super-sonic outbursts it retreated to its lair. Still wet, Karen and I jumped into pajamas and scrambled to our respective beds. Alice's screams echoed up the stairway as she redirected her distemper towards Ed:

"They were still in the tub up there! They should be in bed!"

This was the moment, at age four or five that I recognized I was dealing with something different. Reactions to my actions would likely be delivered with disproportioned severity. Not always more severe, but never quite predictable. This was not "normal" in any sense I had of the world. I would later come to believe we were dealing with some sort of undiagnosed illness. While this was a scary moment, especially for someone my age, it was also strangely instructive. There we were, four people very much ill at ease with each other, living in the same house. We were lucky to have enough space for each to have his or her own room. I never focused on the relationships the other three people had with each other—it was beyond my comprehension. I simply realized that I needed to figure out life by looking through my own lens. Theirs was somehow distorted. I needed to observe a wider range of people to help me learn right and wrong, good and bad, and all the gray area in between. It was a weight I carried with stress and apprehension, but it also became a freedom; a freedom to consciously experience the world through my own filter, and no one else's. That was really a gift.

Tensions varied off and on in the house. We were always just around the corner from the next blow-up. If I ever needed a reminder, it came each night as I brushed my teeth in the bathroom mirror. Over my left shoulder was the reflection of the linen closet door. The splintered knob-sized hole stared back at me. Forty-five years later, the door still remains in this condition, even as the house is being shown for sale. I imagine the next boy occupying my former room, looking through that hole and seeing his whole world opening up.

In between the common events that became hysteria, there were stretches of normalcy. Alice was, let's say "doing the best she could" as we would later call it. At her best you could see her trying to instill some life lessons in us.

Maditude

We were stopping in the local grocery store, Almacs, right around the corner. My father did the weekly grocery shopping there, so this time it was a quick stop for Alice. In the course of shopping I found a folded ten-dollar bill on the floor of one aisle. This was not just good luck, but a fortune for a ten year old. It would keep me in penny candy for a year! Ten dollars at that time would be equivalent to finding a fifty-dollar bill today. My glee soon receded when Alice announced that I needed to take it up to the office, so that if the rightful owner inquired it would be there for them. She followed me up to the front of the store where a small corner was bullpened by high walls and a small window. I'm still curious why the people in the office were three steps higher than the store floor as they stooped to answer inquiries, cash checks, or sell stamps. I followed Alice's instructions and turned in the loot. She interjected from behind me, making sure that my name was given so that I may reclaim the money if it was not spoken for in a week. That was the time period given by the gruff man in the office when pressed by Alice about their procedures for lost and found.

I sweated out the remainder of the working week and then the weekend, hoping the new week would bring my good fortune back. Exactly one week later I presented myself through the office window and inquired about my claim as Alice tapped her foot behind me. The woman now manning the office window knew precisely zero about my inquiry. There was no record, piece of paper with my name, no reward left by the rightful owner, NOTHING. I protested enough to have the woman consult with someone else out of view. Soon the gruff man was back:

"Yeah, somebody picked it up."

"But I left my phone number and nobody called me?"

"Yeah, I said somebody picked it up last week."

Alice interjected: "I'm trying to teach him a lesson about doing the right thing! You people need to keep track of things like this!"

"What can I tell ya, lady?"

Lesson learned, don't be a sucker. My heart sank as both my loot and/or possible reward disappeared. Alice was upset that an impromptu office meeting on the "lost and found" procedures did not seem imminent while I was completely focused on my reversal of fortune.

So that's how a life lesson formed from the observations of a ten year old by watching my parents' behavior and their interaction with the rest of the world. In my case there was a lot of "what not to do" lessons.

Every kid has a fantasy about finding free money on the ground. Mine evolved into a recurring dream. I'm smoking a cigarette behind the Almacs in the narrow dirty alley and find a briefcase filled with mob money. How I know it is mob money is never clear, but when I open the case it's filled with a million dollars in small denominations. Now I know from the movies, TV, the newspaper, even Little League, that mob money is a dilemma. It's not free in any sense of the word. I ponder the situation and arrive at the perfect solution. I skim off a hundred thousand dollars stuffing it into my jacket pockets, and then I turn in the briefcase at the Almacs office. At this point I'm completely satisfied that the "lost and found" process will resolve the situation in one of two ways. One, the asshole in the office steals the briefcase and is hunted down and killed by the mob. Or two, the case is logged in, and later retrieved by two large men who mercilessly beat the asshole over the missing hundred grand. Unfortunately, I wake up on Holland Avenue, out ten dollars and down to my last cherry licorice.

. . . . .

In the winter of our sixth grade year, Stephen and I came up with a new idea. We had watched a full week of our favorite Clint Eastwood westerns on the four o'clock "Dialing for Dollars" movie hour during the winter school break in February. We thought it was our time to kick open the saloon doors.

One of the only perks my father received at the bank was gifts from his customers, usually small business owners in the city. During the Christmas holidays a few customers would give him a bottle of booze adorned with gift box and bow. Neither of my parents were drinkers, thank God. Who knows what that may have brought into the quick-tempered, tension filled mix. Each year a couple of these bottles were pridefully displayed under the Christmas tree and then stored in the back of the linen closet.

It was cold winter evening. The ground was covered with six inches of snow and ice, remnants of previous storms and melts. After the dinner dishes were dried and put away, I checked to make sure no one was in the downstairs bathroom. I got dressed to go out for the evening as I often did. I wore long johns, jeans, flannel shirt, hooded sweatshirt, and army jacket, "Herman Survivor" insulated boots, gloves and hat. I went into the upstairs bathroom and opened the linen closet to reveal three rows of neatly stored gift boxed bottles. I reached to the last row against the closet wall and opened the box and removed the bottle. I removed a piece of clothesline twine I had found in the basement and knotted it several times around the neck of the bottle. I raised the bathroom window and set the bottle against the outside asbestos shingles below the window. I slowly slid the bottle down the house using the length of twine to guide it. It made a slight bang against the shingles and my heart raced. The closer it got to the first floor the less control I had. When it reached the first floor bathroom window directly below me it started to swing back and forth. I could not afford a tap on the window that was sure to alert the first floor residents. I let go of the rope. I knew I could always explain a broken bottle in the yard as a neighborhood drinker's throw over the fence from the adjacent street. I was sure that a detailed inventory of gift bottles was not going to happen.

I went downstairs and announced I was going out with Stephen. I had a ten o'clock curfew on weekdays and eleven on this Friday night and weekends in general. I was out the kitchen door and directly through the open fence gate into the backyard. Crunching through the snow and keeping low beneath the kitchen window, I was amazed to discover the unbroken bottle lying in the snow near the basement window well. I quickly stashed it my jacket and was off to collect Stephen.

We walked the neighborhood streets and turned onto a dead end that housed the tall chain linked yard of the DPW (Department of Public Works). It was filled with pickups, dump trucks, plows, and piles of sand and salt for the roads. At the end of the road four short concrete poles prevented vehicles from continuing down the path from the pavement into the woods. We made our way through some short trails to the park and found a bench to sit on. I revealed the bottle of Canadian Club whiskey to Stephen and he broke the seal with a twist of the cap. He took the first swig and grimaced as he handed the bottle back to me. My first sip was shocking in that I found nothing pleasant in the taste or the fire in my mouth. I swallowed and turned my head to gasp. We passed the bottle back and forth more slowly with each turn, each putting on our best Clint Eastwood expression and not willing to let the other know how horrific the process was. After more than an hour we had nearly half the bottle down and agreed it was all we could stand. Actually, we had quite a bit of trouble standing at all.

We clumsily made our way through the park to the other entrance at the parking lot of Alice M. Waddington. I stashed the bottle in the same shrubs I had pushed Robert Louis Stevenson (yes, that was really his name) into in kindergarten. It seemed a desolate enough setting with no school activity on the weekend.

I remember the continuing struggle for footing as we walked our way back to Holland Avenue. Once in Stephen's backyard we sat at the picnic table in the dark, trying to hush our laughter and falling down repeatedly. After awhile I tried helping Stephen into the side door and down the basement stairs to his bedroom. We remained undetected and I retreated and managed to find my way into my upstairs bedroom across the street.

The next day we met and compared notes. My bed spins and nausea were trumped by Stephen's vomit in their basement bar sink. This had not been completely unnoticed by Stephen's mother, but written off as a food-based episode rather than a drunken twelve year old.

That evening we met up again in the same manner. We went off to retrieve the stashed bottle. We agreed it would be difficult to drink without something to mix it with, so we walked to the local grocery store and I perused the mixer section of the soda aisle. There was club soda, tonic water, and ginger ale, all in glass quart bottles. What caught my eye was the fourth choice, Tom Collins mix. It looked most appealing to a twelve year old because it reminded me of "Fresca." I bought the Fresca and proceeded to dump half of it out, replacing the contents with the whiskey. I had invented a new cocktail, the Whiskey Collins! This concoction was a brown, effervescent, carbonated treat that tasted like dirty socks. We found our spot in the park and began passing the bottle back and forth. Again we finished about half before giving up. This time it was me who was sick, but luckily before making it home. We were drinking men now.

Thirtysome odd years later, Stephen came to my father's wake. As he said hello to my wife Leslie, she said, "Stephen, I've heard some stories about you!"

He looked back at me and said, "I still can't drink that stuff."

# Riva-side

I understood the rule of riding my bike along with the flow of traffic, but the crash in Barrington didn't change my habits. My thought was at least you could see what was coming and try to avoid it. If you rode with the traffic you'd have to trust who's coming up from behind you. In my continuing quest to discover life's rules of the road, I found the church rules to be too strict. I did enjoy a sense of belonging to the community, mainly the basketball team and cheerleaders. I didn't trust the rules made at home. I thought they were overly severe or driven by an irrational fear of the unknown. How was I supposed to learn anything if I avoided the unknown? I discovered the very practical rule of not drinking whiskey until you're older than eleven. I learned this through experience, survived, and obtained the knowledge that this rule is more than arbitrary. See how it works? I also learned that the rules surrounding money vary greatly with the amount and who has a chance to end up with it. That's a lesson for a lifetime. I think I'll take a ride around town and see what else I might learn.

. . . . .

I often think about growing up in Riverside, Rhode Island. My earliest memory is of walking home from Alice M. Waddington School on Legion Way (named for the American Legion hall on the corner), getting past the final crossing guard at the top of Holland Avenue and breaking into a sprint to cover the last three quarters of the block to 160 Holland Avenue. I wasn't racing home to see my family, or the anticipating the lunch I would have after an exhausting half-day of kindergarten. No, I was racing towards my afternoon of freedom. I ran right past the kitchen door of our 1950s Cape Cod-style house, through the backyard to the shed. I retrieved my bicycle, running it back up to the side door and laying it across the concrete steps. It would shorten my trip to freedom. As soon as my tuna fish sandwich was in me I could step out the door, grab the waiting handlebars, and be gone.

On this brilliantly brisk October afternoon, my mother Alice required a jacket, but no more than a heavy flannel shirt was necessary. I tore up the driveway and out onto the street in celebration, sliding to the back of the banana seat until I could lean on the sissy bar and pull the bike into several wheelies. The wind came in gusts that blew brown oak leaves into funnels of small tumbleweeds that you could ride right through.

I thought about the old baseball card clothes-pinned to the rear-wheel-spokes-trick that was common in the neighborhood. When properly tacked on to the wheel, the baseball card sounded like an engine to us. I was thankful I had the constant rustle of the brittle brown leaves instead. I purposely skidded my bike to a stop at the top of the street. The displaced leaves revealed the gray back of a baseball card. I recognized it immediately by the columns of statistics listed below a caption of some little know fact about the player. The card had seen better days, as it seemed permanently warped into the semi-circular shape caused by the repeated strikes of the spokes of a bike tire. I turned it over to quickly look at the player photo before discarding it and was amazed to find Willie Mays staring back at me. Now I completely understood the need for some supplemental engine-like noise to be added to your bike on occasion, but what idiot treated a baseball legend like this! When I used a clothespin and card, it was always a double of a card I owned, or an obscure player on a team of little merit. I would like to add an apology now to Bill Grabarkowicz of the Cubs. I bent back the Mays card into a better shape and stuck it in my pocket. It was going to be a fine day on my long, windy road to freedom.

The streets of the neighborhood were all interconnected. Not a planned community, cul-de-sac to be found. I felt I could go almost anywhere, except downtown, which was too far and blocked by an auto-only bridge across the Providence River. Five blocks away from home and I began a purposeful weave letting the bike fall gently from side to side as I enjoyed the sensation and breathed in the dry fresh air.

A half mile later I looped around the church parking lot. Not a car in the lot. It was a quiet Tuesday afternoon and I took in the beautiful modern architecture of our new tribute to Saint Brendan, whoever he was. The narrow stripes of colorfully stained glass, offset by the brick columns, were really striking from this distance. There was not the distraction of the nails, blood, and thorns on the images you can't ignore from a closer view of the panels.

I can't tell you how I could feel this so succinctly at age five and half, but there was serenity in being alone. I was able to define my interaction with the town, the church, my family, and people in general, to how I imagined it should be.

I rolled past Saint Mark's Episcopal, across the abandoned railroad tracks and down into the square. The square was once the town center of the area in East Providence called Riverside. It now consisted of thrift stores, empty storefronts, a package (liquor) store and the weinie joint. Across the street was Red's candy store, which was my focus for a supply of penny candy. As I threw down my kickstand on my gold Columbia bike, I glanced across the street to the weinie joint.

If you're not familiar with this local delicacy, it consists of a small hotdog inserted into a steamed bun with yellow mustard applied via a wooden dowel, then add spooned-on oily meat sauce, chopped onion pressed on top with a fork, and a shake of celery salt. All this happens to the weinie while being balanced on the hairless tattooed arm of one of the counter guys whose names always seemed to end in vowels. The patrons could be any working Joe on a lunch break, but this time of the mid-afternoon meant just a couple of guys in white T-shirts smoking cigarettes, drinking coffee, not even trying to hide the fact they had nowhere else to be.

When I went in there to order, usually with my father waiting in the car, I'd put on my gruffest five-year-old look, shout out, "Three all the way" as a counter guy looked at me, all the while soaking in the sounds and smells of the place with its counter bar and opposing six booths. There was scattering of these places around Providence, all with old neon signs that said either "New York System" or "Coney Island System." Some people had a preference for one over the other, but I never really found much of a difference. I imagined there must have once been a great rivalry between two conglomerates with a vast network of shops before the Great Depression left these remnants. My three weiners would be added onto the arm of others being made, then wrapped in wax paper and inserted into a brown bag that would eventual bear the oily outline of its contents.

But today it was Red's penny candy store for a stash of Squirrels, Bit-o-Honey's and licorice. The small brown bag slid into my jacket pocket, still open to allow access while I pedaled.

Maditude

As I neared my house on Holland Avenue, I heard the blare of a police alarm starting up. I knew it was close by and I immediately detoured towards the sound. I cut through a small patch of woods across from the school that led to the back of the building that formerly housed the W.T. Grants department store. I made my way around to the front avoiding potholes and broken glass and spotted the flashing lights in the distance. There was a police car, fire engine, and a rescue squad all on one side of the road.

I had gotten there in time to see a stretcher being loaded into the rescue squad. Phillip Warmsley, a kid a couple of years older from the next street over, was strapped to the gurney. His mangled bike lay to the side of a car with some scrapes of yellow paint missing. I got in a close as I could before a cop told me to move back. Then I sat back on my bike seat with my front wheel turned at ninety degrees like I had just settled into the front row of the movie theater. I watched the rescue squad pull away with the full lights and siren. Then the firemen, and finally the police left with Phillip's bike protruding from the trunk of the squad car. I dispersed with the remaining curious onlookers, concerned shopkeepers, wandering souls and headed back to my house.

I was thinking about what a good day it was with the Willie Mays card and the good fortune to witness the action of the accident scene, when I heard the echoing pitch of my mother's voice repeatedly calling out my name. I still cringe at the thought of it. It's rising hysteria. It seemed louder than any of the sirens of the last hour. My face was reddening with embarrassment. How could someone scream like that in public? I pedaled hard into her sight just to stop that noise. It worked as she transitioned into berating me about how she had been calling me earlier and where had I been. I guess she thought I should always be within shouting distance, which would mean on either of the parallel blocks of streets, which was the exact real estate that my bike allowed me to avoid at all times.

I dumped my bike behind the fence into the backyard with the hopes of an after supper evening ride. I hurried through the side kitchen door in hopes of confining the remainder of today's tongue lashing to the house. This went on for a time only interrupted once by my mention of the Phillip Warmsley incident. I was thinking it might generate some diversionary interest in the kid from Becker Avenue. Did I know if he was all right? He was laid up with a broken collarbone, but otherwise fine. My mother showed no interest in this, but managed to use it against me as an example of what danger I was in not being within shouting distance on my bike. After not showing much comprehension, I was finally released from this tirade and told to put my bike away in the rusted aluminum shed in the back corner of our yard. I refused to show any disappointment with this, all the while knowing my diversions from family life that evening would be limited to trying to get a TV picture good enough to follow the basketball during the Celtics preseason game on Channel 4 Boston. If not, it would be *The Honeymooners* on the 12 inch black and white Panasonic upstairs in my room.

The next morning I sat at the breakfast table listening to AM Radio with host Salty Brine's commentary with the occasional song mixed in. This morning I was lost in Petula Clark's "Downtown" hit tune, thinking about how great it must be for my father to work in Providence every day. How exciting and different it must be in downtown.

Providence was the capital city of Rhode Island. It was settled by a group of people, notably Roger Williams, who were kicked out of the Massachusetts Bay Colony by the pilgrims for not following strict rules. From what I could see, the Pilgrims probably had a point. For the most part, Rhode Island's culture was made up of working class-oriented folks who had a pretty large sized chip on their shoulders. People generally didn't smile and say hello unless confronted by family or the oddly awkward neighbor. It seemed that everyone was a rebel of some sort, represented by the "Independent Man" statue that sits atop the Capitol building. I didn't understand what we were all rebelling against if we were all thrown out of the same place. Rhode Island is mostly a very scenic state with quaint villages that line its coastlines and countryside. Today if you visit its two major cities, Newport and Providence, you'll find an attractive mix of history, food, and shopping. But in the late 1960s and '70s, Providence was a much different place. Commerce was evaporating as the textile mills and jewelry making operations had migrated, leaving banking and insurance as the remaining legal businesses.

Downtown had more than its share of empty storefronts and shady neighborhoods. The two largest retail employers, department stores Sheppards and the Outlet Company, had shuttered their doors leaving a large span of the shopping district vacant. Previous generations had famously said, "Meet me under the Sheppards's clock" as a starting point for an evening out in Providence. The clock still remained, but perpetually read ten after eleven, and by 5 p.m. the city emptied leaving an eerie ghost town that continued through the weekends.

The constituency of Riverside, just six miles over the Providence River, was mostly made up of Italian, Irish, or Portuguese families of modest means. The former two held the upper hand in having been there earlier and were able to turn their prejudices from each other to the "Port–a–gees." Since I was half Portuguese myself but with a German last name and lighter skin tone from a chalky English grandmother, I was exempt. The area had its own language shortcuts and thick accent. It seemed everyone had a nickname including me.

Everyone referred to me as "Starz," my shortened last name, but it sounded like "Stoz." The accent seemed to incorporate the worst of both a Boston and Brooklyn accent. A straight Boston accent was much more provincial sounding, like John F. Kennedy's address to the citizens of Berlin during the airlift. He dropped his "r"s but still had an air of aristocracy. When he said, *"Ich bien ein Berliner,"* with a dropped "r," the translation changed from, "I am a Berliner," to "I am a jelly donut." If you can imagine mixing that in with the

guttural shortcuts of a Brooklynite, you get something
sounding like:

"My sista's got wikid P.S.D.S."

That translates to:

"My sister has wicked pierced ears."

Wicked being the universal adverb of the populace,
mean things can be wicked awesome, people are sometimes
wicked smart, and that new guitar is definitely wicked cool.
Now mix that in with some local terminology and you're ready
to order a "Cawfee Reh-ga-la" at the Dunkin' Donuts. But you
need to remember that regular coffee means too much cream,
too much sugar.

"Riva-side" was once a resort area with its Narragansett
Bay waterfront lined with summer cottages, an amusement
park, and a shore dinner and dance hall with a boardwalk. At
one time the boardwalk extended all the way across the bay to
Rocky Point in Warwick. I think its heyday was in the 1920s,
extending into the big band era of the '40s. By the time I came
around, the dinner hall had burned down long ago, the
hurricane of 1938 eliminated the boardwalk, and the bay was
polluted with discharges from oil barges, oil depots, and
sewage treatment plant runoff.

The only time we went near the waterfront was to collect driftwood with my father for some cheap firewood in the winter. The amusement park, Crescent Park, was on its last legs. It did have an influence on my daily life back then, because each report card grade of "A" achieved at Alice M. Waddington, was exchangeable for a ride ticket at the end of the school year. I made sure I had straight A's just for that reason. No teacher was going to jip me out of free rides at Crescent Park.

I finished my breakfast, grabbed my lunchbox and met my best friend Stephen out on the street for the walk to school. I went for the "Topcat" metal lunchbox inspired by the cartoon of the same name. Topcat was the coolest cat in town, so said the opening theme song, and Stephen and I thought we were pretty cool cats even at that age. Stephen lived diagonally across the street from me in a small, low slung, green ranch with his parents and four siblings. He was the youngest and had a head full of ideas; he held the world by a string, benefiting from the experiences of three older brothers. He and I spent almost every day together, sometimes to the disdain of my mother. He seemed to have free rein in their household, always with an idea of something new to try. His closest brother in age was five years older, the same gap as my sister and me.

I can remember riding our bikes, when a summer rainstorm had Alice calling my name to come in. Without his riding buddy, Stephen returned home also, but not for long. Stuck in the house on a Saturday afternoon I left a nose print on the living room picture window as I watched Stephen return to the street on his bike with only a bathing suit on. He proceeded to ride in front of our houses in the pouring rain, splashing through puddles and pulling wheelies in an act that would have made Charlie Chaplin proud. Alice had some choice remarks related to his intelligence and his parents' lack of common sense, amongst other shortcomings. I was completely amused by both the performance and the reaction inside 160 Holland Avenue.

We both liked Clint Eastwood, James Bond, and *The Wild Wild West*. We'd wrestle to the death, then walk to the corner for a soda or to pick up Kent Golden Light 100's cigarettes for his father at the package store. We'd sit in his older brothers, Robert's and Jerry's, bedroom listening to Robert's vast record collection with cool songs like "Big John," "Sea Cruise," Chuck Berry and Elvis 45s. In the evenings we'd sit on the step of Baird's Texaco and watch cars revolve around us through the rotary, always pointing and calling out our notice of a cool Mustang or Corvette.

When we started kindergarten that September of 1967 with 45 or so other kids, it was a tough first day when they divided us alphabetically. Stephen's "N" had him in the tail end of the first class, while my "S" had me squarely in the second group. It probably was the best thing for me in terms of learning, as I was at least a little less at ease for a while. Luckily the schoolwork came easy to me and I soon focused on who to hang out with during recess for some fun. Seated next to me was another "ST," Robert Louis Stevenson. At this point in life I had no clue about the literary reference, or his parent's lack of imagination regarding his name. He was a tall lanky kid with a classic bowl haircut and a prominent overbite with feet splayed like a penguin's.

After a few days of recess camaraderie, and as we were released from our half day of class, Robert challenged me to a foot race down the front path of the school building. The athletic ability Robert displayed at recess could most kindly be described as awkward, so I quickly agreed. He may have gotten off a step sooner, but I found I could not catch up to his long gait and flailing arms and legs. At the last moment I resorted to brushing his heel with my stride, causing a stumble that brought his awkwardness to center stage. He sprawled into a full body skid as I passed him at the bottom of the path.

He stood up and swung his lunchbox in a roundhouse move and caught me on the side of the head. I took this as invitation to wrestle and grabbed him and pushed him into a shrub lining the path. To my complete surprise, he sobbed like an infant. This sort of thing didn't happen wrestling Stephen. Even if his older brother jumped in and you caught a bit of a beating, there wasn't crying involved. Dumbfounded, I walked away as some teacher came to his rescue. How can you hang out with someone who cries when you fight?

After that I focused on hanging around with Stephen after school and was reticent to incorporate any new faces into the mix. This pattern repeated itself several times throughout elementary school as Stephen and I were never in the same class, even when the school expanded to four classes for each grade. Occasionally I would hang out with some other kid for a few days, then decide they didn't measure up, or watch as Stephen intimidated him away.

Stephen was the King of Cool. He knew how to act, look, and behave like he was much older, and I followed right along. I'm sure some of it had to do with having those much older brothers, but also it came from picking up behaviors from popular movies of the time like Steve McQueen in *The Great Escape* and Paul Newman in *Cool Hand Luke*.

That type of entertainment wasn't available in my home. When I finally did get to a movie theater with the family it was *Oliver!* It took me a million miles from Holland Avenue and I was completely absorbed in Oliver Twist's plight to escape the evil foster homes by taking up residence with the "Artful Dodger" and Fagin's band of child thieves. I asked for and received the soundtrack album for our Christmas record player. I even tried out and won the part of "Charlie," master pickpocket in the Alice M. Waddington production a few years later. I was cocky, and already enjoying the company of girls in the play during rehearsal, but on the night of the performance I faded into the background mumbling a couple of lines. Being in the school play just wasn't cool. Even a fourth grader knows that. I returned to my usual antics of getting in to enough trouble with Stephen to keep it interesting without getting my parents involved.

One winter evening my parents visited Waddington for the annual parent-teacher open house. My father begrudgingly went along after some incessant nagging by Alice. He was tired after a long day on his feet as a teller in the downtown branch of the bank. His daily requirements included dinner at 5:15 p.m. nightly, after which he would retire to his chair with the evening paper. My sister and I were required after dinner to clear the table and dry dishes. This was sometimes interrupted by my father yelling about some news from the paper or some item he found for sale in the "Yankee Trader" section. This would be replied to with a shrill, "What is it, Ed!" from Alice that ended the exchange.

This was a complete contrast to Stephen's house where dinner was served several times based on the coming and goings of the adults and elder children. I would be invited to eat over, but seldom accepted based on the inability to navigate Alice's standard objections of, "They already have too many mouths to feed over there" or something derogatory related to the nutritional content of a perspective meal across the street.

On this night of the parent-teacher visit, Ed was instructed to remain in his work jacket and tie, finish dinner quickly, and get up to Waddington with Alice. This was midway through second grade and I had established a pattern of getting straight A's for my Crescent Park ride tickets, along with a less than satisfactory conduct grade of "3." The scale was 1 to 3, with one being angelic, two satisfactory, and three poor. I was usually convinced by my parents into making a two for one of the winter quarters, but always fell back to my three in the spring. They seemed resigned to accept the less than ideal conduct grades in exchange for good academics. A teacher-related event not involving my conduct grades held no real interest to me, so I carried on with my usual evening of TV.

When my parents returned home, there was a look of shock in Alice's eyes, as they reported nothing significant to me other than Miss Flodin's opinion that my studies were progressing well. I would find out much, much later that each parent, during their brief private time with the teacher, was given a numerical rank of their child in the class of twenty-five or so. When told that I ranked three, my parents thought it was my conduct grade again, but eventually understanding when they were provided with the names of the two girls who ranked above me. I guess there wasn't much of an exchange, only bewilderment and a conversation on the ride home about how this could happen. I was a little too young to translate the stunned look into something like pride. Positive emotions or loving sentiments were never spoken out loud in our household, but I had a feeling that was more the norm for our neck of the world and thankfully didn't take it personally.

# Not Gifted

So maybe Riverside didn't provide as many clues to the secrets of life as I had hoped. I escaped being the target of prejudice, but got an up close look at how people used their heritage as a false differentiator to feel superior. I had similar competitive instincts. Whether it was my free ride tickets at Crescent Park, or that early grade school ranking, I was looking for signs that I fit in. With a few bits of positive reinforcement I was starting to imagine myself as a smart, athletic, handsome, popular kid that not even a blow to the side of the head with a metal lunchbox could shake. I looked to popular culture figures on television, in the movies, and on the sporting fields to copy behaviors. There was just one problem. I kept getting not so subtle reminders that my brilliance was limited, my athletic abilities weren't awe inspiring, and I needed some braces on that overbite.

. . . . .

The next summer I finally received the OK to sleep over at the Stephen's. Stephen and I were again inseparable spending long summer days riding our bikes all over town and finding relatively innocuous ways of passing time. The small house across the street was full of activity. Five kids, two parents, and the daily visit from Uncle Freddy, who lived nearby in a converted cottage by the bay, overflowed their three-bedroom ranch with its single bath. Stephen's bedroom was in the finished basement where there was barely enough room for a guest. I was looking forward to this because I knew Stephen regularly stayed up on Friday night to watch Johnny Carson on the *Tonight Show*. Stephen's adult siblings cast some curious looks my way as the evening progressed. They would loudly ask his mother what the hell I was doing there. She replied with a faint disapproval and a roll of the eyes that I was sleeping over. It was obvious that Stephen's will had prevailed. We sat on the living room carpet as Carson delivered his monologue. At a couple of points, Stephen's father chuckled out loud. This was fascinating to me because I had never seen the man smile. When the band played and the credits rolled, I thought I heard an extra voice through the music.

"Oh, my darlin'! Oh, my darlin'!" echoed through the living room screen door. Uncle Freddy soon appeared all smiles. Mrs. N. leaped into action trying to quiet his singing and telling him to get in the house. Freddy was all giggles, obviously over-served at the Knights of Columbus again. This was a real treat for both Stephen and me as we laughed right along with Freddy over the agitated commands of Mrs. N. The only people I had seen drinking or drunk at that point was limited to Ralph Kramden on *The Honeymooners.* We continued our good belly laugh for several minutes before Stephen's mother finally got Freddy to lie down on the couch and be quiet.

Uncle Freddy was really a nice guy with sort of a soft spot for Stephen and me. He could often be talked into buying us something from the Del's Lemonade trunk that circled through the neighborhood in the summer or give us a ride somewhere around town. He was a bachelor and I think he worked at the same BP oil depot operation that Stephen's father managed, before taking early retirement. He did tell us that he had a tryout with the St. Louis Cardinals baseball organization after the war. He was known to be a speedy outfielder with some talent, although he stood about 5'6." Very rarely would you find Freddy in a bad mood, and believe me, he had ample opportunity given some of the stunts Stephen and I pulled. What stood out about Freddy was his car. He drove a new Cadillac Coup de Ville, bright red with a white landau roof, with the license plate FAROE for Frederick Allewisious Roe, his full name.

In our neighborhood it was rare to see a new car of any type driving through, never mind a Cadillac. Not only did the car draw attention to the fact Freddy was at the Nelson's, which was often, but also how he arrived. It was not uncommon to find the Caddy not in the driveway or curbside, but in the travel lane of Holland Avenue as though stopped in mid journey. I can remember finding it one Saturday morning, vacant, down on the corner of Harrington Road as if about to make a right turn. I thought someone would surely smash into it. But it always seemed to be retrieved without any harm being done.

Some years later, when Freddy accidentally smashed the Caddy into my parents' used Buick, that we had paid $512 for, on the curbside. They immediately assumed he was drinking even though it was midday on a Saturday. Freddy had one of those metal locking rods that attached from the steering wheel and hooked under the brake pedal. He started the car without removing it and managed to shift into drive before realizing his steering wheel and brakes were locked. He smashed into the rear quarter panel of our Buick parked ahead of him. We emptied into the street after hearing the collision. Freddy apologized immediately explaining his mistake, offering a check for whatever the repair would cost. I couldn't think of a better way to handle it, but my parents were still annoyed and didn't want to take his offer at face value. They ended up taking his money, but didn't fully complete the repairs.

In the neighborhood many of the kids were at least five years older, so football or basketball games usually involved Stephen and me being added to the end of each separate team, assigned to guard each other. I can still remember Stephen telling me not to ease up when tackling a much bigger opponent because "that's how you get hurt."

Sports were a great diversion from family life at home. My parents being quick tempered by nature would occasionally become so irritated with one another that the screaming matches lasted for hours at a time. These sessions were instigated by my mother, but occurred when my father had listened to all he could stand about a topic, like why he wouldn't ask for a raise at the bank. He was already working a second job, counting in the money room at the horse track on Saturdays. These arguments would escalate during the evening sometimes culminating in some modest physical violence of pushing and shoving followed by door slamming and more yelling. Early on I would hold my pillow over my head and squeeze it to my ears, hoping for the argument to end. Later on I learned that with my door closed, I could avoid the stomach churning angst of their battles by listening to the ballgame on my little black and white TV with a simple set of earphones in the jack. While I always preferred the calm to the hysteria, I believe I developed a kind of immunity to their outbursts. I would always avoid any role in the argument, but really didn't care what it was about or who did what to whom. I felt a certain sense of power in not caring about the outcome.

No one in my household was a sports fan of any type, so I loved the solidarity of it. It seemed like a great way to interact with the greater society without having to deal with live people. It took me far away from the confines of 160

Holland Avenue. I naturally jumped at any chance to actually play sports, whether in the neighborhood or in any organized group. I constantly hung around the older guys in the neighborhood just for the chance they would need an extra guy on one side or another. I read the sports page religiously and watched endless games on TV. I knew more facts and statistics than the average fan. When it came to playing sports, I would not be considered a great athlete by any measure, but I did bring craftiness to it.

Stephen and I spent a lot of time throwing the baseball around and we were both quite skilled with throwing, catching, and fielding balls whether on the ground or in the air. When we started to play Little League, Stephen was picked onto the American Legion-sponsored team, while I was selected for the Giovanni's restaurant team. In Riverside, small businesses sponsored Little League teams for goodwill and community spirit. The Legion team had a collection of good players managed by a younger coach not much older that the guys in our neighborhood, and always seemed to compete for the League title. Giovanni's was managed by Eddie Doyle, a short, tam-o-shanter clad Irishman who also helped with the collections on Sundays at St. Brendan's by working the metal basket on a long stick up and down the pew rows.

Eddie was excitable both during games and in practice. His temper would rise and he did not hesitate to yell at players whose execution was not textbook. For example, one of his proudest couching achievements was how our second baseman would drop to one knee when fielding a ground ball to ensure it did not pass through his legs. We'd spend almost all of our practice time on drilling the basic maneuvers in the field. Throwing to bases, applying tags, backing up plays at bases, etc. We spent very little time learning to hit live pitching. This turned out to be a problem as we generally competed in terms of pitching and fielding but rarely produced enough runs to win games.

I know there is only so much you can do with ten and eleven year olds, but I was having trouble making consistent contact with the ball. In between seasons I even resorted to asking my father for some help. This did not translate into batting practice sessions but rather the advice: "The faster they pitch it, the faster you should swing."

My lack of hitting prowess amplified in my second season. My Waddington school classmates were starting to hit with power and talk about their home runs in class. I was still relegated to the occasional ground ball single. I played a good center field, had a strong throwing arm, and did some relief pitching as well, but as they say "chicks dig the long ball." I could barely stand hearing the classroom chatter about the home run race in school, until one day it changed.

It was a warm, late spring evening and I was manning my usual center field spot at Forbes Field, which was on the highway connector to Interstate 95 in Providence. One of my classmates was batting for the opposing team and hit a deep fly ball to right center field. I raced into the gap between the right fielder and myself, angling back towards the 3-foot chain link outfield fence. I followed the ball in the air and eased my angle as I neared the fence. Being right-handed meant that the glove on my left hand was already on the ball side of the play. I reached for the ball, which snared in the webbing of my glove at the same time the top bar of the chain link fence hit my side. The impact wasn't too bad because of my shallow angle and I managed to hang on. I turned back to the infield and threw to the second baseman, out onto the outfield for the cutoff throw.

There weren't that many people around but I did hear some clapping led by none other than Eddie Doyle himself.

The next day at school all the chatter was about how I had reached over the fence to rob John of a home run. I finally had a little bit of glory and didn't have to beat it out of anyone. Years later when Eddie Doyle was knocking on neighborhood doors in a successful run for Mayor of East Providence, he related the story to my parents, saying it was the best catch he had ever seen. I smiled broadly as my parents said they didn't remember it happening. Even to this day when I'm back visiting the old neighborhood and drive by Forbes Field, I mention to anyone who will listen, that it was the sight of the greatest catch in Little League history. Whether it's an old friend or my wife, having heard the story more than once, they roll their eyes and wonder out loud why they haven't renamed the field in my honor.

That same year the town Little League expanded with a new team sponsored by a local men's clothing store, Ray and Nick Creations. They were a bit of a rag tag group with an inexperienced coach and a team full of players taken from other teams or new to Little League. It was one of the few teams we beat regularly. The funny thing about it was they had nice new equipment and uniforms, and regardless of the negative outcome of their games, they always were treated to ice cream afterwards. I think we had ice cream twice that year, once after a surprise win and another time after the last game of the season. I secretly hoped for the first trade in Little League history.

The ice cream benefactor, Nick Sr., was the father of a team member and my Waddington classmate Nicky. Nick Sr. was the same Nick of Ray and Nick Creations and he took the kids to the creamery after each game he attended win or lose. Nick handled the tab by stripping off bills from a thick roll held together by a rubber band. He was a friendly, outgoing guy always dressed in a suit and tie, from his clothing store I guessed.

Later in the season at our game against Ray and Nick Creations, Nick had his suit jacket draped over his shoulders due to his right hand being bandaged. I remember him shaking hands with one of the fathers with his left hand. I didn't think much of it, and after the game their losing side was off to the creamery again.

His son Nicky was a classmate of mine for a long stretch as our last names were in the same part of the alphabet, though we were never close friends. He was a nice kid, but quiet and kept to himself more often than not. Six years later in high school we were still alphabetically linked for a homeroom attendance period, when a story broke in the local newspaper, the *Providence Journal*. Nick Sr. had been indicted in the mob slaying of Joe "Onions" Scanlon. Through of series of reports during the ensuing trial, we learned that Ray and Nick Creations was a front for the mob and that "Ray" was the crime boss Raymond Patriocca Sr., head of the entire New England mafia based in Providence. It seems that Nick was holding Joe "Onions" head while an associate of Nick's was shooting Joe. Nick was accidentally shot in the hand. While there seemed little doubt, according to the evidence relayed in the newspaper, that Nick was guilty, I flashed back to that Little League game years before and the bandaged hand for my own corroborating evidence and felt lucky that Nicky Jr. was not the kind of kid you got into fights with. Nick Sr. was convicted and drew a long sentence at the ACI (Adult Correctional Institution) in Cranston.

Someone that I did get into fights with in grade school was Bobby. Now Bobby, if you're out there, please take this as a half-hearted apology. You really egged me on; it was as if you dared me to fight with you. I thought he must have had a very short memory because the fights always ended badly for him. I'm not sure how many times per week, but at least once, I would pummel Bobby into tears on the playground.

When I ran into him much later in life he asked me if I remembered beating him up every day at school. I really don't think it was every day, but I did have a temper and he really did dare me to do it. Not a proud memory. The way things played out at that point in school, Stephen was known as the toughest kid and I was his second. I couldn't have Bobby talking trash in class everyday without consequences. When I look through old school photos there seems to be a contest between Stephen and me over who scowls better. He probably won, because mine had a hint of a smirk as well.

. . . . .

My sister Karen is a speech pathologist today with an undergraduate dual major from the University of Rhode Island and a graduate degree from Western Michigan University. I tell you this now, because early on at Alice M. Waddington things were a lot different. My senior by approximately five years, Karen was sent off to school with the same type of nurturing and social skills you might imagine were ingrained from being in our household. Not only was she a bit unsure of herself, but also had the added hindrance of an undetected eyesight problem. Her grades were not good and she was actually held back a grade until finding a helpful teacher in Mrs. Perry and a good pair of glasses.

I was much too young to comprehend this at all, but cannot forget the screaming and yelling at home. My parents were convinced that she just wasn't trying, or that she was trying to get bad grades. How the yelling and belittling could possibly help her was a mystery to me. I think these memories, added to the Crescent Park ride tickets, were incentive for me to do well in school. Fortunately it didn't take much effort and left plenty of time for me to screw around. Karen was more than indignant that things were much easier for me, and you wouldn't blame her if you had heard the ritual screaming she had to endure.

My parents' outlook on life seemed to set them up for some eventual collisions. My father was generally well liked and was competent in his work in the bank. He worked an extra job in my early years to help make ends meet. He loved the outdoors and had a passion for fishing. He was also a bit high-strung, evident in both the occasional outbursts of temper and the frenetic schedule of Saturday chores that routinely resulted in losing Sunday to a stress headache. He liked to travel and experience new things, but was mostly limited to non-headache Sunday car rides in the country.

My mother was beyond tightly wound and had a wary way of interacting with the rest of the world. She worried incessantly and would much rather stay at home and complain about chores to be done, than partake in anything new and potentially enjoyable. There was always a reason not to do something that often reached beyond the budgetary constraints into irrationality.

Some of the conflict between Ed and Alice certainly came from their opposing view of the world. Alice was always distrustful of new people, places, and ideas and imposed her views in a combative manner. Ed was more resigned to his lot in life with a young family, modest means, and a reluctant mate. He seemed to lack the energy for many of the verbal jousts with Alice over relatively minor decisions. Growing up with this backdrop, and being more aware than the average nine or ten year old, had its challenges. Given that, I can't say any of my decisions, whether ill conceived or occasionally insightful, were overly influenced by my parents. I did have this yearning for something different and a willingness to try new things and I'm not sure where I got this curiosity from—definitely not my dear parents.

The summer after fourth grade was spent on my bicycle with and without Stephen, or in the driveway shooting baskets. For my birthday in June my Uncles Jesse and Johnny put up a basketball goal at the end of our driveway. It was not quite right, but their hearts were in the right place. They sunk a square wooden post into the ground with some gravel around it and mounted a painted plywood backboard at the top. The post really needed to be anchored in concrete, as the wood post would flex and return a shot with more force than usual. This was tempered by the plywood backboard of less than regulation width, which did not have rigidity required for the proper reaction from the ball. It was all topped off with a sturdy rim, that unfortunately was mounted an inch or two too high.

The previous winter I had begun playing in a Saturday recreational league at the Oldham grade school near the Square in Riverside where my Uncle Jesse was the janitor. At that age I had pride in the fact that my uncle was the one who would let the players, coaches, and the occasional family member in to the gym on Saturdays and sweep the floor prior to the games.

He and his wife Aunt Mae were also my godparents from my baptism at St. Brendan's years earlier. Aunt Mae being Alice's eldest sister by more than ten years, seemed more like a grandmother to me. Jesse and Mae, not having children of their own, paid special attention to Karen and me. On Saturdays Jesse would delivery extra groceries to the house and I would help carry the bags in from the truck of his mint 1962 Chevy Nova.

Stephen and Tommy, another neighborhood kid a year younger, liked to tease me about the extra groceries. Tommy I simply beat up, but Stephen's comments rang a bit truer as I knew there were many things about my family that were "not cool."

I liked my Uncle Jesse, cool or not. He was a baseball fan and we always had a brief exchange about the state of our beloved Red Sox. The Sox were on an extended non-competitive streak, which began right after I started in kindergarten when they lost the World Series to the St. Louis Cardinals in the full seven games. Barely understanding the significance of the World Series at age five, I did know one thing. "Yaz" was the man. Carl Yastrzemski picked up the Red Sox and carried them into the playoffs with a historic

September hitting display that culminated with him winning the 1967 American League Triple Crown (first in batting average, home runs, and runs batted in) and the Red Sox winning the pennant on the season's final day. He is still the last player to accomplish this feat in either league (until Miguel Cabrera of the Detroit Tigers in 2012). Five years later the Sox had not been able to assemble a complementary squad to compete in their division, let alone a chance for a pennant. Uncle Jesse's commentary on the Sox ultimately ended with his catch phrase, "they're a bunch of hams."

It was also an eventful summer in that it was the last for Crescent Park. This old girl had seen better days and was sold to developers who began to tear it down for the construction of low-income housing. There was a mild public reaction that was rightfully centered on the carousel, which was harnessed by a fleet of hand carved wooden horses by a well-known German craftsman. It was spared and still stands today as a memory of a very different time in Riverside's prosperity. Now, having my main motivation for achieving good grades removed might have been worrisome for many, but I soon realized that the competitiveness at my core was not controllable.

The next school year Alice M. Waddington would provide all the motivation I needed with the introduction of the "gifted" program. Suddenly during the fall term new classmates were sprinkled throughout the four classes of the fifth grade. These kids were from Rumford, the more successful northern part of East Providence, which included two country clubs and easier access to downtown. As students we had no idea what this was about, only that one period during the school day these kids were collected for a class with a special teacher.

They were an odd collection of kids, some with questionable hygiene habits and introverted personalities. It seemed like no one washed their hair or changed their clothes. It was not a club I was looking to join. What did irritate me was the time they got away from class. When we did discover it was the gifted class, it didn't even occur to me that none of my regular classmates from Riverside were in the program. I did later find out that the parents of both the girls ranked above me in first grade had inquired, one vehemently, about participating, and were both rejected. I'm not sure what testing or evaluation techniques were used, but I was happy that my parents could not fathom any giftedness in me and spared me the reject status. I was even more jubilant when we non-gifted students were exposed to one of their "projects."

We were taken up to their special gifted room upstairs to watch a poorly staged, amateurish production of *The Crucible*. Not only was regular class time better spent with Ms. Duffy's serial reading of the classic book *Johnnie Tremain*, but I was also avoiding this embarrassing display by the "most likely to be hit in the face with the kickball" players. *Johnnie Tremain* is a 1943 award-winning young adult novel by Esther Hoskings Forbes about a boy, injured while working in Paul Revere's silversmith shop, who turns to newspaper work and becomes intertwined in the Revolutionary War. I loved hearing that story unfold each afternoon and for years held onto the idea of journalism as a career. It was like seeing twenty minutes of a movie everyday as the images jumped from the pages into my mind. Ms. Duffy deserves the credit for introducing me to the power of good books—*Johnnie Tremain* was my gateway to adult reading and was followed by Ms. Duffy's reading of Dickens' *Great Expectations* during the spring term. I still regret that I never went back to thank her and let her know what a difference she made.

There was a gifted student who came along in either fifth or sixth grade that stood out in the fact he was reasonably athletic, well-groomed, and smart: Patrick Toomey. By this time I had started playing basketball for the Saint Brendan's CYO team and Pat played for the Saint Martha's parish in East Providence. I think my mother Alice knew Pat's mother from high school. Anyway she would often interrogate me about goings on at school and seemed to bring up his name more than most. I said as little as possible, as was my policy, but there really wasn't much to report regarding Pat. I knew I could beat him in basketball. That was the only imperfection I could find as he was generally at the top of the class in everything.

One snowy day our sixth grade teacher Mr. Travers, my first male teacher and a sports fan to boot, allowed us to play tackle football on the snow-covered field out back. As we scored our first touchdown, none other than Pat Toomey shouted a challenge to its validity. I said something unpleasant back. As we kicked off, I decided to seek him out on the play and deliver a crunching block. As I ran towards him he recognized my malicious intent and jumped up delivering a cheerleader-like forward kick, which unfortunately landed in a very sensitive area. As I writhed and rolled on the ground, Mr.

Travers approached, asking what was wrong. I stood up, lifting my head towards the teacher and said:

"Fucking Toomey just kicked me in the fucking balls!"

"What!!!" screamed Mr. Travers, and the game was suddenly over.

Mr. Travers' eyes widened and he yelled for me to get up against the school building wall where I remained until the students were sent back into the classroom. I was then marched to a desk set up in the hall outside the classroom with Mr. Travers taking a seat directly across from me. He leaned in to grab a hold of my shirt collar in order to threaten me with parental phone calls, expulsion, or anything that would come into his rage-filled head. The rest of the class could see and hear everything because the open layout meant only two bookshelves divided the classroom from the hall. They were silent with folded hands. I think I managed to say "no" to one of the questions about whether I wanted to be suspended, but I never got to ask the question that I really wanted the answer to. Sure, teachers should not be happy to be addressed using that language, but what about Toomey and his unsportsmanlike girl kick? In all of my probationary period that followed the incident, I never laid a hand on Pat Toomey. Pat moved on to parochial school, followed by Catholic high school and then on to Harvard.

Thirty-five years later, my wife Leslie and I were watching the national election results on TV. When we saw the newly elected U.S. Senator from Pennsylvania I said:

"I think I went to school with this guy, Pat Toomey."

She asked, "Is that Fucking Toomey?" Sure was.

While I think Pat may turn out to be a very competent senator, I still don't think he was "gifted."

# Scrappy

What I learned at this mid-point in grade school was that I was tougher than the smart kids and smarter than the tough kids, but I really didn't stand out otherwise. This meant that the inverse was also true. I didn't possess a natural instinct to excel with either group. I was highly competitive, but didn't always channel it in a positive pursuit. I was very aware of my surroundings and was actively looking for clues on how I might fit in. While I was waiting for this discovery to present itself, I'd protect myself with a layer of attitude. If I believed the recreational league clippings from the East Providence Post, I was on the verge of becoming a standout basketball player at age ten. I just needed some time for my athletic abilities to blossom and channel them into my natural sport, whatever that may be.

I can't overestimate the impact sports had on my life in Riverside. I watched almost every sport intensely and revered the Olympics. I loved the changing and overlapping of the sporting seasons and their associated playoffs and championships. No one in my house had any real interest in sports. To me it became a connection to the wider world. You could exchange impressions of last night's game with the neighborhood kids, or with other adults who you would not have otherwise interacted. Watching sporting events brought me out of Riverside and into sporting venues from all over the country and the world. I would watch motorcycle racing on ice tracks in Russia, or Track and Field events in Europe on ABC's *Wide World of Sports*. I loved the Olympics, especially in those days of true (unpaid) amateur athletes. I soaked up the back-stories of the athletes and truly enjoyed the background reporting on the local culture and history of host cities. I was so adamant about watching these games and events that a typical 5:30 p.m. Saturday dinner at home often included the TV cart rolled into the hallway. I would eat at the family table with my head turned ninety degrees to view the culmination of a game.

My own athletic abilities remind me of a baseball commentator's description of a player as "scrappy and versatile," scrappy as in he can't hit and versatile as he's not good enough to play one position. That may have fit, but it didn't dissuade me from participating.

I played organized baseball until I was fourteen when I chose to retire from my version of the Bad News Bears. I don't remember the team sponsor's name or uniforms, but early into my second season I knew my time was up. We were coached by two well-meaning fathers who were the far from disciplinarians. Our unsupervised rookie batting practice consisted of the 15 year olds throwing at the rookie 13 year olds, and I do mean "at." During games we had signs from the bench for certain situations. When we were on base, the steal sign was when the coach picked up a bat. Unfortunately our coach liked to chat with parents and spectators in the adjacent bleachers, and often picked up a bat to lean against. We unintentionally ran our way into countless double plays and out of big innings.

My contribution to this mess was getting picked off first base because I was watching the pick-up basketball games over my shoulder on the nearby court. The sound of the ball hitting the first basemen's mitt brought me back to the diamond from the basketball court where I would simply walk back into the waiting tag of the first basemen on my way to the bench.

Once an older teammate took over the third base coaching with signs that included picking his uniform out of his butt. I can't imagine what this team looked like from the stands, but an appropriate team sponsor might have been Bradley Hospital, a local institution specializing in children with psychiatric issues.

One summer during grade school Ed and my Uncle Jesse took me to Fenway Park in Boston. I had been following the Red Sox since the 1967 World Series appearance and chatted with my Uncle Jesse each week about their progress. The Sox had settled into pattern of non-competitiveness in the American League, mostly due to poor pitching. It had been five or six years since the "Impossible Dream" season of the World Series.

Our trip was not stress-free as Ed navigated the fifty miles of driving into Boston with heavy traffic. I was relieved when he eventually found parking for the Sunday game at a closed gas station, although the five-dollar fee seemed exorbitant.

We filed into the old brick façade on Yawkey Way and made our way through green painted concrete corridor. I bought a program for thirty-five cents. We found our section number painted on the steel beam above a set of concrete stairs. I could see blue sky in the distance. As I stepped into the opening, with the field and stands revealed below, a permanent photo was snapped in my mind. The field was a beautifully manicured, and bright, bright green. Green painted grandstands and the famous "Green Monster," the thirty-foot wall and historic manual scoreboard surrounded it. This was offset by the infinite rows of red wooden slatted seats. It gleamed in the full sunlight of the day. I was overwhelmed. After having watched so many games on television, most in black and white, it was like having a painting come to life. The day lived up to expectations on the field as well. The Red Sox dominated the dismal Milwaukee Brewers winning 9-0, behind the legendary pitching of Luis Tiant "El Tiante," and a grand slam by Rico Petricelli.

Stephen and I played sports with the older kids on the block whenever we could. Once, we were added to a neighborhood team playing a tackle football game set up against kids from Barrington. I soon realized this was more of a grudge match than a normal game in the neighborhood. I wouldn't be going out for a pass, or touching the football in any way. That was reserved for the older, more skilled players trying to assure a victory. I was relegated to blocking and tackling. The Barrington kid lined up directly across from me, trying to rush our quarterback, repeatedly told me he was going to "kick my ass." Tackles in this game were sometimes accompanied by punches. I never hit harder than on that day in the vacant field next to the old barn in Barrington. No monogram sweater-wearing, swim and tennis membership, chip off the old block, Barrington kid was going to kick my ass. I fought off the bigger kid all day and even bloodied his nose with a stray elbow.

We were the kids from literally the wrong side of the tracks, tracks that ran through West Barrington separating it from Riverside. We thought Barrington kids were soft and privileged. This view was passed down to the younger generations. For Stephen and I, it was one night when we were eight and sitting on the concrete steps of the Baird's Texaco station. A Mustang convertible pulled in to the pizza shop next door with a loud group of Barrington teenagers. The driver, a big kid dressed in loafers and a sweater around his neck, was particularly loud. There were a few of the non-sweater wearing, local kids in the parking lot. Words were exchanged:

"Why don't ya go back to fuckin' Baaaaarrrington!"

The Mustang driver volleyed something disparaging back and a confrontation ensued by the take-out window. Not much more than finger pointing and pushing took place. Then a Riverside kid name Dana got involved. He was wearing overall jeans without a shirt, displaying his muscular torso. He got up off his motorcycle, removing the lock and chain from the seat handle, and walked up to the now re-occupied Mustang. There was a quick exchange of words that we couldn't hear. What we did hear was the sound the chain hitting the windshield and spidering the glass. The visitors wanted nothing more to do with this and screeched across the lot, heading straight from where they came. There were no police called, no particular fury of emotion, just a comment, "I'm sure Daddy can afford a new windshield." And that's how it was for most of us regarding our sentiments towards Barrington.

. . . . .

Like I've said before, my interest in basketball started in CYO leagues. I played and practiced year round in playgrounds, gyms, and even the driveway after shoveling snow. I'd purposely take the wrong bus home from middle school to the housing project that replaced Crescent Park. Their playground was active and I could get in a game with the help of the familiar face of a classmate. I'd make the long walk home or get lucky and have somebody's parent give me a lift. I kept playing basketball well into high school until my ability no longer matched my size.

Ed noticed how much time I spent playing basketball and after a few years something nice happened. One of his bank customers, a season ticket holder for Providence College basketball, sometimes gave Ed tickets to less popular weekday games. We'd go down to the Providence Civic Center after dinner to watch the Friars beat the likes of Brown University, or Fairleigh Dickinson. I enjoyed the basketball games. Providence had a good team and had made the "Final Four" of the 1973 NCAA Championship. It took me out of the neighborhood and into an environment where I observed people's rituals. It seemed people could treat basketball as a social event by attending with the same group of friends, talking about the game afterwards, and maybe stopping for a beer at the pub. This camaraderie wasn't far from Oscar Madison's poker games on *The Odd Couple*. We would only watch the game and leave, but I could see my future self fitting in to some group of happy sport fans, devoid of the angst and worry at home.

One of my favorite diversions at home was watching *The Odd Couple* on television. Early on it was shown in primetime on Friday nights following my sister's choice of *The Brady Bunch*. A few years later it was in reruns and frequently found on the 12 inch Panasonic in my room. Anytime there was turmoil in the house, I'd retreat up to my room and into the Manhattan apartment of Oscar Madison. In this alternate world everyone understood the importance of getting to the ballpark. Sports stars of the day were referred to by commonly known nicknames. Oscar, played by Jack Klugman, was a sports reporter by trade. His activities were portrayed as going to games, eating ballpark food, smoking cigars, drinking beer, chasing girls, and meeting famous athletes. He was a notorious slob. I could not imagine a more blissful existence. His live-in nemesis was Felix Unger (Tony Randall), who was a finicky, fun hating, clean freak. Oscar and I had more than the love of sports in common. Sometimes I'd steal lines from the show and try them on Alice. She would be yelling about the state of my room:

"Why can't your room be clean like the rest of the house? You can eat off the floor!"

I'd counter with one of Oscar's lines from the show:

*"You can eat off the floor in here too. Look, there's a slice of pizza and here's a half a tuna sandwich,"* talking as I pointed to imaginary items on the floor.

This would get no reaction because the mess in my room could only consist of dirty clothes, no food remnants were allowed. After she retreated, I would get great joy out of the joke by somehow connecting my room with Oscar's.

. . . . .

The last summer after finishing our time at Alice M. Waddington, Stephen hooked me up with my first job. He had somehow found his way on to the maintenance crew at Seekonk Speedway. Seekonk was the neighboring town just across the Massachusetts border. The speedway was a paved oval short track that hosted races for Class-A Modified (think of a souped up Chevy Vega), down to Street Division (un-modified) and the occasional Demolition Derby. I was picked up at 5:45 a.m. on Sundays by a guy named Louie and driven to the track to pick up trash. The seating at the track stood partially on paved ground by the entrances and midway concessions. The grandstands on the far side were bleacher benches on dirt and gravel. The maintenance crew had a homemade vacuum truck that sucked up trash from the paved area with a wide hose. The dirt and gravel on the far bleachers was our territory: a small group of kids, with a nail on a stick and a trash bag, would comb the dusty bleachers. The whole place smelled like a mix of stale beer and body odor. The odor hung in the dew, and then evaporated into a foul mist as the temperature of the summer mornings climbed.

Mr. Vandetti owned the speedway and would oversee the cleanup operations from the announcer's perch above the grandstands. The permanent crew was a group of Portuguese men who did not speak English. Early one Sunday I was walking a full trash bag to the dumpster and as I passed the vacuum truck loudly sucking its way down a section of seats, the men operating it looked up and started yelling:

"Domp-a! Domp-a! Domp-a!"

I didn't understand what they wanted and certainly couldn't ask a question above the roar of the machine or in a language they would understand. My dumbfounded expression resulted in some hand gestures as they approached with the vacuum hose. This was little help, as I couldn't fathom pouring out the full bag of trash I had just picked up. One of them grabbed the bottom of my bag lifting it up to empty the contents as the other sucked the trash with the vacuum hose. As the process finished I released my grip and the plastic bag itself sucked into the hose. This caused a problem I didn't see coming. When the bag went up, everyone starting yelling again, this time joined by Mr. Vandetti from above. I guess the plastic bag was not good for the vacuum machine. Louie had to settle Mr. Vandetti down in order for me to keep my job that day. I guess I was supposed to know about the operation of the vacuum truck from the training classes and the review of the OSHA regulations we received? I made a mental note not to make this job a permanent career choice.

The mornings always ended in a positive way as we were paid eight dollars in the track office and then piled into Louie's Mach I Mustang for delivery back to our houses, but not before a free breakfast at the Friendly's restaurant on the way. So this is the working life. You have to get up very early, put up with some bullshit and bad attitudes, but you get paid and can eat what you want. Lesson learned.

I returned to the speedway for a job the next summer with working papers in hand. This was my first official job. Since my age was documented and met the minimum, I would be able to work the Saturday night races as well as the Sunday morning cleanup crew.

My first Saturday I was sent to the French fry concessions stand on the midway. It was a wooden shack about the size of a small shed. Inside there was a fryer, a small heat lamp, and a counter that ran beneath a sliding window where patrons would place orders. One shelf held the supplies of paper cups, napkins, and plastic packets of condiments. Near the fryer was a cooler with sacks of frozen French fries. In the middle of all this stood Ray. A small man in his late forties wearing a wife-beater tee shirt, Dickies work pants, and steel-toed black tie shoes. He turned around to reveal a heavy beard, and sallow skin already shining with perspiration. A lit cigarette was wedged into the corner of his mouth. He smelled like he had come from the Sunday morning cleanup detail. My arrival was met with only a grunt. I was given a cursory overview of the price list and cup sizes, and pointed to the calculator and the gray strong box with petty cash.

As customers approached I got the hang of taking orders, typing the total amount on the calculator, making change, and sliding a cup of fries from under the heat lamp into their hands. The napkins and condiments, sitting on the counter, were up to them. This all seemed reasonable to me. I was anxious for the crowd to grow to avoid the awkward silence inside the shack.

With the darkness of the night came a hungry crowd, which turned into long lines queuing up for French fries. Ray frantically increased the fryer output to its maximum while shouting for me to move quickly. I tried to keep things running while remembering to type each amount on the calculator. When one of the sizes would run out under the heat lamp, Ray would cannibalize the remaining sizes to fill the order. Our frenetic pace did not wane for more than two and half hours. Later, still during the rush, a customer asked me for an additional empty cup. I was pulling one from the stack when Ray suddenly intervened, grabbing the cup and telling the customer we weren't allowed to give out extras.

The lines dwindled during the last half hour between ten thirty and our closing time of eleven o'clock. At eleven we switched positions. I was assigned to clean the cooking side, draining used oil and wiping down the counter. Ray counted the money in the strong box, hit the total button on the calculator and tore off the tape. I finished up and went to the rest room. I returned unnoticed as the speedway manager was in discussion with Ray. Evidently the count between the French fry cups and the cash was off. There were more cups missing than the cash sales predicted. I tried to remember if I'd throw any away during the rush as several had fallen on the floor.

The manager's accusative grimace moved from Ray to me as he declared, "This will be docked from your pay."

Ray's head shook with the disgust of a disappointed parent. I thought, how much can cardboard cups cost?

Then I realized they were assuming I sold extra cups of fries and pocketed the money. How had Ray managed to avoid suspicion? Shouldn't his pay be docked? I guess that's why he was the cook, not the cashier. So if I follow along with the logic of the concessions manager, on my first day I outmaneuvered a mean short order cook; gamed the system to avoid recording revenue; and pocketed the cash. Either that or I schemed with a transient cook to pull off the great French fry robbery! The heist plan must have had me taking the fall. How much could they dock my $2.55 minimum wage check anyway? It was only $15.30 for the night's work. Another valuable lesson was learned that day. Just because they're in charge, it doesn't mean they're smart.

I managed to keep a job at the speedway that year, but never again in the French fry finance department. They kept me on and gave me the responsibility of holding a whistle. I reported out to the parking lot, where an odd man on a bicycle appointed me to a location and gave me instruction on directing cars into the parking lots. The front of the speedway had a paved lot with parking spaces, which held about a third of the expected Saturday night crowds. The only other paved lot was behind the track and reserved for the pits. The remainder of the customers needed to be guided down grassy two-tracked paths to the surrounding fields that served as overflow parking. Our supervisor would ride his bike between sections, moving our positions and handling any snarls. Every so often a driver would ignore my whistle and hand gestures, seeking a shortcut. I would try my best to keep order, but race fans hardly cowered at the sight of a kid with a whistle. Many of these shortcuts turned into encounters with soft sandy patches that left cars stuck in their tracks. Drivers would curse as they tried to rock their cars back and forth onto solid ground, sometimes only succeeding with a helpful push from my supervisor and other drivers.

Occasionally I would be assigned the parking section that included the pits. It was my favorite as I got to direct the trucks and trailers into their assigned spaces in the pit area. It required a pit pass for entrance into the fenced lot behind the track. Once inside, I became more useful as newer drivers and crewmembers would ask me about locations or the facilities in general. This was the first sense of pride I had about being employed. It also came with an unforeseen benefit.

On one Saturday night I noticed a group of fans lined up along the far chainlink fence that separated the pit area from the grandstands. They were mostly women and as I walked closer I could see them all staring in the same direction. A few hundred yards away, standing in his race suit talking with his crew, was Paul Newman. He resided in New England and was known to occasionally race at a similar track in Thompson, Connecticut. He was a serious driver and wanted nothing to do with the celebrity seekers. I'm sure he would have signed autographs, but only in pit row after a victory. Later in the evening I was able to say hello when walking by his pit crew, but there was no chatting.

Watching a movie today means a choice of the movie theater, cable TV, Pay-per-view, On Demand, rentals by mail or kiosk, internet streaming, etc. Our choice back then was television. TV in most cities consisted of the four networks, ABC, NBC, CBS, and PBS; in Providence that translated into channels 6, 10, 12, and 36 respectively. You would click the round dial to the channel number and experiment with the set's top antenna until the picture became clear. For PBS, you needed to set the dial to the "U" setting for UHF (versus VHF dial which only had channel numbers 2-12) for the alternate frequency and set the second dial to channel 36. You would then manipulate the second, round antenna for a clearer picture. The portable set in my bedroom had the advantage of the second floor and received stronger signals. I had watchable picture quality from the Boston stations fifty miles to the north. The equivalent Boston stations were 7, 4, 5, and 2, with PBS being on the VHF frequency. The NBC Channel, 4, was the home of Celtics basketball broadcasts with Len Berman and Bob Cousy calling the games. It's hard to imagine now, but the local affiliate chose to broadcast the basketball games rather than the network's primetime line-up. In addition to these channels, Boston offered two UHF channels that were independent, non-network affiliated stations, channels 38 and 56. Channel 38 was the home of Red Sox baseball and Bruins hockey games. Dick Stockton and former Red Sox player Ken "The Hawk" Harrelson called Red Sox games. I spent many hours, close to the set, trying to follow the action through the snowy signal reception.

On evenings when there wasn't a game scheduled, *The Movie Loft* with host Dana Hersey was standard fare. Dana spent a few minutes introducing each movie including background on the stars, directors, studios, and time period of the film. He would often include his opinions on what made the film significant above and beyond the awards it may have received. His manner was friendly and casual, matching his attire and hairstyle from that time in the early and mid 1970s, but his baritone voice gave added weight to the film-watching experience. Dana was like a friend at the bar telling you a good story about something you both enjoyed. There wasn't a bar in my room, but on the set of *The Movie Loft* you'd often find Dana leaning over the loft rail talking directly to you.

*The Movie Loft* incorporated themes into the movie line-ups. Some weeks focused on particular stars, directors, or a type of award winner (cinematography, costume, best picture or director). It was during a theme week that on consecutive evenings Dana introduced Paul Newman's work in *The Hustler*, *Hud*, and *Cool Hand Luke*.

*The Hustler* was first up with a great supporting cast of Jackie Gleason, George C. Scott, and Piper Laurie. It is the story of the young talented pool player, Fast Eddie Felson who challenges the great Minnesota Fats (Jackie Gleason) to a high stakes match and loses. The remainder of the film is spent with Eddie struggling to find his way through life and back to his previous level. His decisions along the way come with consequences for both he and his girlfriend. It never really works out for Eddie. What resonated with me was that talent alone was not enough to succeed. The choices you make along the way have a lot to do with the outcome; you really can't rely on others to honestly help you make the right choices.

In *Hud*, Newman is in the title role as the anti-hero. He's cool and aloof, which is attractive to the younger characters, but his selfishness is obvious to the older ones. His drive to succeed in life is paired with a complete disregard for others. Hud eventually gets what he wants, but not without causing pain for everyone else. It's not really a success he can live with. It left me with a feeling of wanting to succeed, but not at the detriment of others. I still feel this way.

*Cool Hand Luke* is on the favorite films list of many and a lot of you know the plot and can probably quote dialogue like:

"What we have here is a failure to communicate."

Or

"Taking it off here, Boss."

Or the line that gave the film its title

"Sometimes nothing is a pretty cool hand."

Besides the obvious attractions of a classic film and cast, I connected with Luke's unstated sense of not belonging in his place. He had returned from the war and was having trouble relating to his life at home. He rebels by knocking the heads off parking meters in a drunken folly. After he's imprisoned and put to work on the road gang, he's not willing to follow the rules he's subjected to, regardless of the cost. I was discovering a similar feeling in my gut. It was a feeling of dissatisfaction with my place in life, and the strong urge to rebel.

The next fall I entered Riverside Junior High School and found myself reunited with Stephen at the beginning of the first day. First period began with a very stern woman wearing glasses, a long skirt, and the layered clothing of an old maid, entering the room. Mrs. Macalister explained how things were going to be different. The school was starting an "accelerated program" and our class of thirty and a sister class were the first students in the program. We were restricted to a set of classes that would be more demanding to prepare us for college. She said she expected a high level of maturity and academic achievement. It seemed as though fun would be strictly prohibited.

I looked around and saw new faces from other elementary schools, but also some students from Alice M. Waddington. I guess if we weren't "gifted" in grade school at least we were worth accelerating in junior high. My wary gaze returned to the dour face of Mrs. Crabby Mac-No-Fun and thoughts of a year without smiles.

Later I did discover one smiling face. It rested atop the six foot five frame of the Assistant Principal in charge of discipline, Mr. Jenkins. Below his salt and pepper military style brush cut were a set of friendly eyes that were never dissuaded by his daily dealings with student misconduct. If you were walking the halls or queued up for class and saw him coming, you could always count on a pleasant exchange.

"Mr. Jenkins, Mr. Jenkins," you would call out.

"What's for lunch today?"

His smiling reply was always the same.

"Oh, delicious, delicious!"

Since home life didn't include many smiles, I'd have to figure out how to get some out of this new systematic approach to my education. It would take some time, but I had some ideas that would hopefully keep me on friendly terms with Mr. Jenkins.

# Vichy French

My plans for becoming a professional athlete were strongly embedded in my imagination. At the same time it became more and more difficult to ignore the reality of mediocrity. I held on to the notion of sports being central to my eventual vocation by channeling Oscar Madison, the fictional sports writer. My initial foray into the working life came with mixed results while strengthening my resolve to try to find my own way. Work had introduced one more source of people telling me what to do. The list of which included, family, school authorities, coaches, and classmates, was already too long for my liking. As I began junior high school, this seemed to get worse. I imagined what it felt like to be in occupied France during World War II. Life's terms dictated to you by Nazi-controlled institutions at every turn.

It was Bogey week on the *Movie Loft* when I learned about the Vichy government of France during the Second World War. After Germany had conquered France and occupied Paris and large portions of the country, a collaborative French government was set up under President Henri Petain to administer the non-occupied areas of France and its territories such as French Morocco. This is the backdrop for the story in *Casablanca* and my favorite movie *To Have and Have Not*. Both the Nazis, and the corrupt Vichy officials oppress the characters in these films. The latter film is the adaptation of the classic Hemingway story with the screenplay written by William Faulkner. With the ever-present tension at home and the new strict environment of junior high academics, I felt a natural connection to the characters.

At home things were slightly improved as we had graduated from the days of being hit with the belt and Karen being kicked up the stairs during rageful fits of punishment. It's not as though we didn't deserve punishment at times, but it was the wild temperament in which it was delivered. As we all got older you could sense a level of fatigue with our previous mode of operation. What remained were tightly wound personalities that sometimes exploded into fits of yelling and screaming. The physical part of the household relations was now thankfully in the past.

Alice was often distracted by her workplace traumas. She had learned to drive and had gained employment in various offices doing clerical work. My father had more than urged this during arguments about his low pay at the bank and his goal to give up his second job at the horse track. Alice's experiences with working followed a pattern we would all come to loathe. It always began with a honeymoon period where she would enjoy some aspects of the new job. But as she learned more about the office and her co-workers there would be an inevitable conflict that was painted as an epic battle between good and evil. Alice would talk incessantly about an often-minor interaction with a co-worker or boss, repeating it in the exacting detail of her point of view. She would literally stew over a particular incident, talking to no one in particular about what she should have said or done, and what she was planning to do about it in the future. She would wind herself up to the point of not sleeping well for weeks at a time. We would all suffer from the resulting moodiness. She would threaten confrontation with the offending parties or quitting outright, but it was usually months, sometimes longer, before she took any action. When she did eventually confront people at the office, whom I imagine wondered what she was referring to, the outcomes were never satisfactory. This would result in the cycle repeating and then her eventual quitting of the job "to get some rest." She would complain about always being "run down" and we would get by without the extra income for a while. I have no knowledge of medical or psychological diagnosis standards, but I believe she suffered from something under the broad category of depression and we all suffered along with her. Alice not only had a high level of anxiety, she was a carrier.

At school the subjects had evolved from my automatic A's in math, English, Social Studies, etc. to Algebra, Literature, Civics and French. We were restricted from selecting certain subjects and classes that were easier. Previously I'd be happy to know the information and regurgitate it on tests, but these teachers wanted much more classroom interaction using writing to display our newly gained knowledge. I felt that was going over the line. School needed to be more of a distraction and I required some fun in the equation. During class I didn't spend time with Stephen, but with the other kids sitting nearby. I talked with the other boys, some whom were baseball fans, and got them into an early version of fantasy baseball. I wrote out the rosters of all the major league teams and brought them to school in my notebook. I handed out teams to four or five kids, making sure to include their favorite, non Red Sox teams. We began discussing rosters like general managers and making player trades. This gave us a diversion from our classwork and content for notes to be passed and considered during lecture time.

Stephen remained stoic with a couple of other boys on the opposite side of the assigned class seating. This was not a "cool" activity. But after seeing the amount of fun we were having and with no alternatives to the strict march of study topics, they joined in as well. After a couple of weeks we expanded again. This time we went co-ed as a few girls could not resist the temptation of note passing and breaktime chatter. It was eventually broken up by a math teacher who heard the buzz in the room when a neophyte general manager proposed a lopsided trade breaking up the great Dodger infield of Garvey, Lopes, Russell, and Cey. The teacher intercepted the proposal note, but had to ask the class what it was. We were told to desist, but no visit to Mr. Jenkins was required.

All three years of junior high included studying French. I could not fathom how this could be important and of any use in my future. I complained about it at home once and Ed couldn't seem to come up with a practical use for it either. A very strict French woman taught us in a language lab. As class began every day she would call us to order with:

"*Bonjour, mes élèves.*"

Our required response was:

"*Bonjour, Madame.*"

To which came:

"*Comment ça vas?*"

Replied with

"*Ça vas bien, merci.*"

Not only did I have to say hello, but when asked, "How are you?" I had to reply, "Well, thank you." I was not "well" most days in French class. Some days I was disinterested, "*désintéressé,*" some days I was sick of this shit "*malade de cette merde,*" but we hadn't gotten that far in vocabulary and we weren't allowed to be anything but well!

One day, one of the special education students got loose and started driving a teacher's car around the triangular drive that connected the main road to the school building. He really picked up some speed as he weaved from side to side, only stopped by a blown tire from the impact with the curb. This was really something to see and I raced to the language lab windows facing the action, followed by most of my classmates. Our teacher resorted to English as she screamed at us to get away from the windows. I tried to ignore her to see the culmination of the incident on the road below, but she kept on screaming. When we returned to our seats she scolded us again saying, "Don't go near those windows, from outside it looks like feeding time at the zoo!"

Now I understood that she was more concerned about appearances, not some lapse in conduct on our part. It reminded me of Bogey's half raised hand and mocking "Heil Hitler" in the Gestapo office in *Casablanca*. It was really about appearances.

Each day we were drilled with French vocabulary followed with the cry, "*Repeter!*" which the class did in unison. The same ritual was followed when we had the headsets on with the man's voice reading from our textbook "*Sans et Sen*" by Scott Forsman and Company. The fact that I still remember the book publisher tells you how many times we were forced to "*repeter*" this process. We goose-stepped our way through sixteen chapters of this *merde* throughout the school year without a smile appearing anywhere in that language lab. I felt like Captain Renault was interrogating me in the Casablanca police station. In the future, whenever I was asked if I had studied French in school. I would reply, "Yes, Vichy French."

But the joke was on me. After three years in junior high, and only needing two years of a foreign language for college entrance, I was told one of the years had to be at the high school level! Another year of French awaited me.

. . . . .

Vacation, like eating out, had a different meaning in our household. Eating out meant McDonald's, which suited me fine. Restaurant meals were too expensive for us. Our only other restaurant experiences were a few weddings. Vacations for my father meant he would have some time off to do chores around the house, like painting it, mixed in with some day trips to the beach or fishing at nearby lakes. I was happy to go along on the swimming trips and avoid the painting at all costs. The next summer we were in for something different. Ed had talked Alice into a weeklong rental cottage on Cape Cod. It was a small place on the grounds with a landlord occupied main house on the inland part of the outer Cape in Eastham, Massachusetts. The location, away from the ocean or the bay, made it affordable for us, and its position on the narrowest part of the Cape meant convenience to both bodies of water.

I looked forward to any trip outside of the neighborhood and disruption in the routines of 160 Holland Avenue. I packed up some clothes along with swimsuits and a jacket and ball cap, and scraped together some spending money. Ed and Alice packed up beach blankets, towels, and sunscreen, and readied the green cooler with cans of dry ice and groceries. It was a very warm Friday evening in late June and our 1972 Dodge Coronet was backed into the driveway, packed and ready for our two and half hour ride to Eastham Saturday morning. Our rental was Saturday to Saturday and we could get into it at 2 p.m.

Ed was anxious for an early start to avoid the heavy bridge traffic on Saturdays when most weekly rentals turned over. I didn't realize how anxious until I was awoken in the middle of the night, 4:15 a.m., and told we were leaving. Alice said:

"It's too hot to sleep, so we may as well get going and beat the traffic."

I don't remember any traffic because I sat in the back seat holding in the nausea of carsickness through the pre-dawn and early dawn hours. It was a long two and half hours, followed by sitting in the parking lot of the Eastham General Store waiting for it to open at 6 a.m. They were expecting the usual fishermen buying bait, but that Saturday they got a family of four killing time, examining every item. Ed and Alice used to recall the trip by saying, "Remember when you used to get car sick?" I'd try to tell them I was never "car sick" again when traveling at normal times of day or night. After quietly driving around the small town and past the rental property street, our next wait was in a bay beach parking lot until opening time. We spent the rest of the morning at the beach, and then checked in at the cottage.

Feeling renewed by a swim and an early lunch, I got my first real look around the area. We drove a mile to the National Seashore Visitor Center to get a weekly pass to the Atlantic side beaches. We continued east through the Seashore to see Nauset Light and Coast Guard beaches. The next morning I emptied out of the backseat into the parking lot at Coast Guard beach and into an impressionist painting of seaside bliss. The wind blew waves through the dune grass as high clouds shadowed the panoramic views of the crashing sea. The Coast Guard House sat high on a bluff watching the Atlantic take back the beach one wave at a time. Surfers unloaded their boards from roof racks and pick-up beds and struggled into wetsuits. A heavy sea mist climbed the dune cliffs as the haze of the sun tried to evaporate it. The few early beachgoers below were flying kites that seemed to dance just out of our reach from the perch above. I welcomed the constant whistle of the wind as it made conversation impossible. I could feel my breath dive deeper and muscles relinquish their grip on my shoulders.

You get a sense of peace when confronted with nature's beauty on a grand scale. I have never forgotten the feeling that day. I felt it often on the Cape through sunsets over Cape Cod Bay or while witnessing the amber tint of morning light over a marsh and meadow. We spent our week mostly swimming and cooking out evenings on a small charcoal grill. The tensions of home life were mitigated through the distractions of this new environment with its inherent beauty. Yes, Alice would complain about the unpacking and laundry that would be required when we returned home, trying to advance a calendar that I wanted to stand still. I learned a lesson there, get out and experience nature whether in the local woods or a national park. The scale of its sensory outputs will make your own world seem insignificant along with your stack of worries.

Back in Riverside I spent the remainder of the summer riding my new Schwinn Varsity ten speed bike and working at Seekonk Speedway on weekends. I found my new bike capable of greater speed and distances, allowing me to climb the long hill into nearby Seekonk for the occasional movie. At dusk I would pedal through the parking lot of the new Ann & Hope department store and into the side alley. Under cover of the darkening sky I could borrow an empty milk crate outside the delivery doors and squeeze through an opening between two fences into the Seekonk Twin Drive-In. I would simple set the crate down on an empty parking space hump, sit down and turn on the metal speaker hanging from its pole. I was far enough from the snack bar, and screened by the size of surrounding cars, that I never had a problem.

We had seen *Jaws* during our trip to the Cape in the small theater in Orleans, Massachusetts. *Jaws* was set in a New England seaside vacation town very similar to Orleans, which made the film even better. I continued to find movies more than entertainment. The best had the power to transport you to new places and observe new people that might give you insight into how the world really worked.

The following fall back at junior high, fighting the malaise of perpetual boredom with my studies and the anxieties that waited in the after school hours, I found a new distraction. A friend and fellow French student brought in some homegrown weed. We smoked it before school in the woods that led to the athletic fields. It was mild in its effects, but had a powerful pungent odor that penetrated every pore and fabric. We must have smelled like we had just cut down the woods with sickles when we entered the school's halls. A few students gave us a knowing glance, but nothing more. The day went by quickly and I felt relaxed in both body and spirit. It felt like I had a protective layer around me that neither anger nor anxiety could get through. Unfortunately the layer was a cloud of odiferous smoke that happened to be illegal.

While I could never be considered a serious student, I always managed to get good grades without taking work home. That seemed to be a reasonable equation for me. I would be bored with subjects and the stiff presentation during the school day, but I needed the time after school for entertainment. If this equation became imbalanced because of issues at home or teacher expectations of greater workload, I would fire up a joint and let things fall where they may. Sometimes my classroom behavior was clownlike, other times pensive and thoughtful. It was a mood of the former that gave me the idea to strip the burrs off bushes in the woods during PE class and bring them into algebra. When the teacher turned to write on the chalkboard, I would throw a weightless, sticky burr at his back that stealthy grabbed the polyester fibers of his sports coat. I think the inventors of Velcro must have been watching that day. I would repeat this process until the chuckles from students would lead him to discovering the disruption.

Christmas approached, as did another installment of "doing the best we can." Christmas had evolved from the joy and surprise of a little kid, to overcoming the complaints of arduousness shopping. Alice would repeat the shopping tasks she needed to do like my French teacher drilling in new vocabulary. We still overcame it and were excited to give and receive in the good spirits of the day and usually would make it into the evening, cheerfully appreciative of the gifts and goodwill. Later, Alice would start to wonder out loud why she was so tired, eventually answering herself with the chore list of the day. If this did not receive enough recognition, we might be treated to daunting account of what had to be done the coming week:

Exchanging gifts

Taking down the Christmas tree

Decorations

Cleaning

Laundry

Ironing…

It was clear sign to retreat to my quarters if I was to preserve my own holiday cheer. You can see me now heading upstairs for an *Odd Couple* rerun or maybe an old movie. I wasn't lacking for anything tangible, food, clothes, bikes, and even sports equipment. What I wasn't allowed was to feel good, or good about myself, at least not for very long. My sister, now in high school, could see the light at the end of the tunnel. For me, the tunnel was too long to contemplate. I would need to find new ways to pass the time.

I was able to secure more regular employment bagging groceries at the Almacs in Barrington. Karen had been a cashier there with a good track record and the same store manager must have thought I might be too. I managed my savings into the purchase of a used dirt bike and joined Stephen in riding through the woods, trails, parks, farms, and even cemeteries. We knew the law said that we couldn't ride dirt bikes on the city streets. Any time we were trapped by pursuing cops we would walk the bikes on the streets back to our houses, breaking no laws. We always started out riding on the streets to get to the woods and trails that could connect us to larger spots in more rural areas. One patchwork of wooded trails took us through Reed's farm where the proprietor was known to shoot rock salt at trespassers. That route also included a higher risk crossing of a divided highway with an escape path through the Catholic cemetery.

Once when riding the train tracks in Barrington we found a police car and mirrored sunglass-wearing sheriff, blocking the tracks at a crossroad. Stephen downshifted quickly into a U-turn and I followed suit. He wound through the gears as we raced in the opposite direction to avoid being cut-off at another crossroad. My less powerful bike could not keep up, but I was able to get past the next crossroad and into a park that connected to woods by the DPW depot. I avoided capture and was walking my bike on the main road next to Almacs when the Barrington sheriff drove up. Without any evidence of wrongdoing, I simply explained I was legally walking the bike back to my house. I knew he had no jurisdiction in Riverside and he let me continue to walk home.

Stephen and I had other diversions that summer: mainly smoking pot in the evenings in those same woods. He had a job cleaning up the meat cutting room at another grocery store. We would meet after work and walk into the park after dark. One night shortly after extinguishing the bowl of a small wooden pipe, we heard footsteps in the park. We turned to see the scanning beam of a flashlight connected to a patrolman, less than a hundred feet away from our spot on a bench. We turned the opposite way and ran down the path. We were stoned, running on an undulating dirt path in complete darkness. I fell over an unperceivable rise in the path as Stephen staggered ahead of me. We heard the quickening footfalls of our pursuer. The path ended abruptly at the ten-foot high chainlinked fence surrounding the DPW garage and yard. We scaled the fence like burglars but encountered three rows of barbed wire across the top. With no alternative, we swung ourselves over the top, but not before tearing both clothes and skin. We dropped into the DPW yard full with sleeping dump trucks and front loaders, scurrying across the yard and in between two trucks. We squatted and leaned against the massive tires to avoid detection from the flashlight beam scanning the grounds from the park. We didn't move for what seemed like the better part of an hour. Eventually we scaled the gate fence and dropped onto the gravel driveway. The gate didn't have the barbed wire on top, so it was a painless vault. We straightened ourselves out and continued our night walk, probably looking for something to eat.

Back at Riverside Junior High for the start of a new school year I found biology on my schedule, not a subject I was naturally drawn to. Our teacher, Mr. Capaldo, was stern, fit, and military in both haircut and clothing choice. He carried a wooden pointer with him when he wasn't actively involved in demonstrating behind the large lab table and sink. Now that I think about it, the facilities at our junior high were pretty nice with language and science labs and other classrooms with amphitheater-style rising rows of desks. Mr. Capaldo lectured us on the basics, filling the chalkboards with notes. There was no talking allowed. My reaction was a typical mix of boredom and resentment of his authoritarian style, but a funny thing happened along the way. I started to find the material interesting. There was usefulness in knowing how something works. And having some hands-on visual props, like the frog we dissected, brought it to life. I still rebelled against the rigidness of his approach, but found he had a greater tolerance for me now that I was making As on his exams. Don't get me wrong, I was still the student most frequently hit on the back of the legs with that wooden pointer. He seemed to appreciate that I was learning, and I actually looked forward to his class and getting whacked with the pointer. I was one of four students who took a voluntary Saturday field trip with him down to southern Rhode Island.

We met him at school on that Saturday and climbed into his Volkswagen Bus, headed down to Washington County, where the University of Rhode Island had its Oceanographic Campus, to explore the marine habitat of tidal pools. On the ride down we learned that Mr. Capaldo was a SCUBA diver and a surfer. I was happy to get out of town and into a new natural setting. We had covered some information regarding the importance of ecosystems in tidal pools in class, and now we would be observing them first hand.

We started in our sneakers and swimsuits wading into the shallows and being shown the fiddler crabs and other creatures in the food chain. Later, Mr. Capaldo brought out snorkeling gear for each of us to use in the deeper areas of the pools. I had always loved the water. It was our main recreation outside of the neighborhood, thanks to Ed. Surprisingly, Alice was afraid of the water. We had never seen her with more than wet ankles our entire lives. I completely enjoyed the tidal pool excursion. Did I mention the other students were three of the prettiest girls from class? Two of the three were quite buxom and I really enjoyed the ride home. Four of us crammed in the van sitting on towels in wet swimsuits, cold skin touching cold skin. I'd had a couple of girlfriends in junior high, but found it hard having only school time and the occasional party to hang out. There was never a chance of bringing a girlfriend to the house. Now I was surrounded with opportunity, but probably a bit out of my league. I certainly had no skills for a multi-girl situation, but still had fun clowning around during the trip back.

I learned from my biology class experience. I found in Mr. Capaldo that I could tolerate being told how and what to do; if it was something I enjoyed doing. In the past I would have reacted badly, displaying my bad temper. Here, I was finding pleasure in exploring new things. I loved the water, especially in its most natural setting. And I really, really liked girls.

. . . . .

In the Catholic Church there are milestone life events called the Sacraments. I didn't study very hard in Catechism so I can only guess that there are seven sacraments and I can only name five: Baptism, First Communion, Confirmation, Marriage, and maybe Death. I think becoming a priest is one of the other ones. Ed was raised Protestant and had little interest in churchgoing. He used to quote his father who complained about attending mass:

"Why does the priest get a full glass of wine and I only get a sip?"

So as I approached the Sacrament of Confirmation, it was solely to satisfy Alice. I took the afterschool class required for preparation and even then it required a home visit from Father Hunt to warn of my imminent failure if I did not buckle down. Confirmation marks the passage into adulthood in the eyes of the church, and requires you to display a certain level of knowledge of the church's teachings. I managed to slip by and received my Confirmation on schedule in ninth grade.

I told Alice, now that I was an adult in the church's eyes, I should decide whether I would attend mass. In a rare display of compromise, she relented saying she had done her bit by getting me Confirmed. The rest was up to me. After I received Confirmation I was handed a letter along with other symbols of my achievement. When I got home I realized it was a letter from my parents. We all received this as part of the ritual guided by the priest who oversaw the Confirmation process at St. Brendan's. I glanced at the letter's contents and immediately became uncomfortable. I put it in the desk drawer in my room, locked away for another time when I was ready to try to understand it.

I really hadn't given much thought to what Ed and Alice's sentiments were regarding me. I knew the basics of clothing, feeding, caring for you when you were sick, keeping track of your whereabouts, were all part of the equation, and more so with Alice than Ed. How they felt about this wasn't a mystery. If that letter had said I was a nuisance, a financial burden, an underachiever, spoiled, lazy, slovenly, etc. I would not have been surprised; what it did say was that they loved me and were proud of me for achieving my Confirmation, amongst other things. I was genuinely surprised and a little choked up by the thought of it. Then I wondered if it was a form letter from the church. OK, I know that sounds harsh, but you have to remember that there were no signs of affection shown in our house. The only physical contact was in anger or sickness. The word "love" was never uttered and didn't manifest itself in any perceivable way. I didn't even believe they liked me. I think the best word for our relationship would be that we tolerated each other.

So for a day or so I thought that they felt differently and just didn't have the ability to show it. It must be another case of them doing the best they could. When Alice asked about the letter, I just said, thank you. For a few days I was a bit confused until some inconsequential incident set Alice off in a tirade of hate directed specifically at me. These outbursts affect you more severely if you believe the person doing this "loves" you. You must really be a worthless piece of shit if this person feels this way. Imagine what rest of the world, that doesn't love you, thinks of you. It was actually a bit upsetting. She made me feel bad about myself again and the only person that should have felt bad was Alice. I went back to my desk drawer, retrieved the letter, and tore it into a hundred pieces and dumped it in the wastebasket. I vowed never to let my guard down again. I learned another of life's lessons. Love isn't what you write down, things that you're not even capable of saying. It's what you do that counts.

As ninth grade turned to tenth any wind of optimism in my sails died into doldrums. The cheerful environs of junior high were replaced with dark and dreary halls of East Providence High School. It must have been designed before the invention of natural light, since none of it seemed to penetrate into the building's gray-bricked interior and yellowed tile floors. What made that first year even worse was the overcrowding driven, split session schedule. As tenth graders, our twenty-minute bus ride began at 10:40 a.m. leaving us on the school grounds with half an hour to kill before first period at 11:35. First period was a study hall in the school cafeteria because no classroom space was available until the juniors and seniors concluded their school day at 12:45 p.m. We used the classrooms from 12:50 p.m. to 4:45 p.m., and then reboarded the waiting buses for the ride home in wintertime darkness. This left me with enough time to work the evening shift at the grocery store three nights a week and on Saturdays.

With all that dead time prior to school each day, came the opportunity to kill the senses with a good dose of reefer. Stephen and I, along with a regular couple of classmates, found places to partake on and off the school campus each morning. Sometimes we would buy it on the front walk under the clock tower, or join with other associates who were flush and whom we could reciprocate with on another day. If we were really pressed, one of our schoolmates had a ready stash from "Ma Turner," his mother the dealer. On special occasions we might have girls join us, who were usually more interested in getting high than hanging out. We might be behind the shopping center across the street or around back of the auto mechanics and auto body repair vocational school building. Maybe even out in the athletic fields that were in clear view of half of the classroom windows.

This daily ritual would get you through the dead, first period, study hall and one or two of your classes, leaving you to grind out the remainder of the afternoon shuffling between rooms in the dark halls like patients in a geriatric ward in the asylum. The school year lasted forever and so did this pattern of coping with the boredom and depression. The only benefit was to my bank account, which started to grow with savings for college, although more school was the last thing on my mind.

With the end of the school year came a welcome change of routine. My grades had suffered with my lackadaisical approach to an all-time low of Bs and Cs. I picked up more hours at the grocery store for the summer. What didn't change was the after work activities of hanging around town stoned. Two high school stoner buddies now regularly joined Stephen and me. These two were quite a pair, with their matching brown leather jackets over T-shirts and jeans. They spent time rehearsing their tough guy sneers in the mirror of their affluent little cul-de-sac homes. They came from two of the most well off families in Riverside, on the newest built street. My biggest problem with the pair was they were dumb as stumps. Stephen and I may have made some questionable choices, but there was an underlying intelligence that came through in our schoolwork and how we saw the world. My brain was also preloaded with an imagination for different life, maybe in another place. These two struggled in school and with common sense. We clashed on a recurring basis.

We were wandering around town after work one June evening with our usual stash of weed. With school out for the summer, I was tiring of the routine, thinking there must be more to do now that the cloud of high school had temporarily lifted. I was with Stephen and Dumb and Dumber when it struck me. I decided not to partake in the pot smoking. As the joint or bowl was passed among us as we walked, I said, "No, thanks." I got some expected haranguing by the idiots, who obliged. They kept harassing me to partake in the weed throughout the evening, which just made me dig my heels in harder. I was not willing to be told what to do by a couple of morons. If I didn't feel like getting high that evening then that was how it was going to be. I told them to "fuck off" several times and considered punching one of them in the face to shut them up. If a fight did break out, I would be fighting both the morons. If Stephen jumped in on my side it would have been over quickly, but he seemed to favoring their side of the argument and even tried to throw in a bit of peer pressure for me to acquiesce. These guys didn't know what tough was. Should I fight them all, just to prove it? I got madder and decided to peel off and head home. What they didn't realize was that would be the last they would see of me. Nobody was going to tell me what to do if I didn't want to do it. That included Ed, Alice, or my outlet from them, Stephen, and certainly not these two dimwits. After a few days of quiet from both sides, I didn't return phone calls from Stephen when they came. I would be on my own from now on. I didn't speak to him again for years and then only a brief comment in passing. *You know what tough is? It's fuck everybody; I'll handle it on my own.*

Why did a seemingly insignificant event create such a strong reaction from me? Was I channeling Alice? Was it genetic and the silly string chromosome involuntarily took over? I think it was the vision that this was all there was for me in life. That I would spend my days hanging around like a townie, with nothing better to do. That picture clashed strongly with my imaginary, future, independent life filled with new experiences, people, and places. I couldn't tell you how, or where this would happen, but I wouldn't let anybody tell me it wouldn't.

A funny thing happened 25 years later when I was back in town visiting. Leslie and I had taken Ed and Alice out to an inexpensive local Italian restaurant and on our way out to the car after dinner, there they were. Dumb and Dumber with the same brown, zipper front leather jackets, leaning against the brick wall outside the restaurant. I had to look twice to make sure. Should I go over and re-introduce myself, maybe with a straight right to the nose? On second glance, a wave of empathy washed over me. These guys were still pathetic. It looked like the pinnacle of their life had occurred when I had last left them. They were still trying to look tough hanging on the corner. If they were really tough they would have tried something different, maybe even took some risks, put themselves in an unknown, uncomfortable situation, and see how they did. The corner would still be waiting for them if they failed.

The soundtrack of my previous few years had been the mid 1970s traditional blues-based hard rock like Aerosmith, Led Zeppelin, ZZ Top, mixed with Bob Seger and Boston. We would ride around with our newly printed driver's licenses and cassette decks blaring through a cloud of sweet smoke. I like to remember that time as my Bad Company period, for obvious reasons.

I learned an interesting lesson about myself. If I'm in a position where people take for granted that I'll make a certain choice based on my own self interest, like staying with my longtime friend and hanging with the supposed cool kids at school, I'll do just the opposite, usually in direct conflict with my own self interest. I'm addicted to the feeling of ripping off the Band Aid. To saying the fuck with everybody, I'll figure it out myself. It's not about starting all over again, but a dreamer's chance that the future might just turn out better. It's really the possibilities I like thinking about. It's the lottery ticket that's worth the dollar, for the plan you make in your mind for what will happen when you win. For me it was time for Plan B. One slight problem, I didn't have a Plan B.

# Do Much Fishin'?

I'm not sure whether it was my first view of Cape Cod, or snorkeling in the tidal ponds with Mr. Capaldo's biology class, but I learned I felt something special being in and around the water. In my search for a picture of the future, could I see myself as a biologist or oceanographer, or maybe an angler? Ed used to bring an older kid from across the street fishing with him. Maybe I should be going along instead? I'm probably a natural waterman anyway. These excursions turned out so well, I considered calling this chapter "How I Became a Golfer."

I was attending a wedding of a friend of my wife's years ago and was introduced to the father of the groom. After a hello and an exchange of names, our host departed leaving us in a moment of uncomfortable silence.

"Do much fishin'?" He blurted out.

"I used to." I said smiling.

That was quite a conversation starter and reminded me of Ed, whose small talk technique was similar and often restricted to basic automotive repair or fishing. Early on I was interested in seeing what attracted Ed to fishing and wanted to tag along on impromptu trips over to the Brickyard Pond in Barrington. We would park on the roadside by an old gate and walk up a grassy two-track road into the woods to get access to the pond. After a couple of times when I entangled valuable stringers and lures in nearby shrubs, or looked down to see a bird's nest of line gathering at my reel, Ed was less enthusiastic about my company. I could see he wasn't getting his usual relaxation from the sport, and his relaxation was much more useful to me at home than a trip to the pond. I went along less frequently but enough to refine my skills and become less of a distraction. I especially liked to go to places that were new to me, or on the warmer summer days when we might be able to take a swim if the fish didn't cooperate.

In the winter Ed would be in his living room chair with the newspaper and call back to the kitchen about some boat and trailer listed in the Yankee Trader section for only $150. The idea, immediately dismissed by Alice, allowed Ed to dream of warmer weather and of days spent on the water. Ed was a WWII navy veteran and always kept his affinity for the water, sometimes without a healthy fear of its more dangerous aspects. He would eventually buy a 3.5 horsepower outboard motor from Charlie, his ex-boss at the bank. It was too good of a deal for even Alice to object to. This enabled more fishing days because he could rent a skiff for five dollars a day instead of "Boat and Motor $14," so said the sign at Wallum Lake in Burriville.

It was 4:30 a.m. in the dark and rain of a pre-dawn spring morning when Ed woke me in my room upstairs. The day before I had told him I wanted to go with him on his trip down to Stafford Pond in Tiverton. It didn't seem like such a good an idea at this moment. It was one of the more pleasant rides down the Narragansett Bay shoreline. Stafford Pond also promised more action to a bored 12 year old because the spawning small mouth bass hit our bait often and sometimes jumped in the air. In the front seat my eyes silently strained through the blur of windshield wiper streaks and the fog of the early hour.

We rented an aluminum boat and bolted on the Johnson 3.5HP motor and were off into the middle of the pond. It was too early for the sun and warmth required to fish the swallows for the spawning small mouth bass, so we trolled the center of the pond for trout. After an hour sitting in the bow with rain puddling at my feet and not a bite on either of our lines, I again questioned my lack of judgment. In another hour I would remind myself never to agree to go fishing again.

Finally we gave up on trolling and moved closer to shore where I decamped to water a shoreline tree. I washed my hands in the lake in preparation for the highlight of the day; the sandwich packed in the small cooler onboard. Back in the boat and before our lunch break, Ed had a bite on his line. As he set the hook and began reeling, a small bass jumped from the water. I now had some action and readied the net as instructed, careful to submerge it into the water gently and not swoop and scare the fish. Ed had another one on the line a few minutes later and I even caught one before we paused for lunch. We continued fishing the same area of good fortune after lunch and netted three more bass. Ed put each fish on a stringer, a chain of separated clips for the gill of each fish. He clipped it to the stern, allowing the fish to tread in the water behind the boat. Keeping the fish alive during the day meant fresh fish for dinner and skeletons for the raccoons to forage for in the garbage can that night.

After a while the action subsided. There were no bites for half an hour and Ed decided to try another shoreline spot of willow trees and lily pads. He pulled the starter cord and the outboard motor purred to life. We cruised across the middle of the lake towards our next spot on the opposite shore. Along the way I heard a rattling noise. When Ed eased the throttle approaching our new spot it grew noticeably louder. Ed cut the engine. When I looked back our wake was full of chum like were fishing for the Great White shark of Stafford Pond. We had forgotten to pull in the stringer and it was sucked into the prop, mutilating our fish and bending up the aluminum stringer. The prop was scratched, but we avoided any major damage. The raccoons would be disappointed that night.

Later in the summer I took the 50-minute ride down to Point Judith with Ed for another fishing excursion. Point Judith jutted out into the Atlantic on the southern coast of Rhode Island and along with its sister peninsula Galilee formed a major harbor. The harbor was flanked by a series of beautiful natural beaches that I secretly hoped we would visit after a short foray into fishing for flounder in the harbor.

We were again sporting the 3.5HP outboard as we rented a wooden skiff from a proprietor found among the lobstermen, charter fishing captains, and people lining up for the next passenger ferry to Block Island. We loaded the gear into the boat and headed out through the red and green buoys of the busy channel into the harbor. I noticed we were the smallest vessel out there and more importantly the slowest as the outboard really strained to push the heavy wooden boat. I tried to focus on the sights and sounds of summertime on the Atlantic coast. Sailboats crisscrossed the harbor. Powerboats of all varieties headed out to join them. Returning lobster boats carried grizzled men with their early morning haul. Seagulls squawked as they followed fishing boats hoping for a stray fish or bait they could dive for. The harbor was vast and protected by the giant reaching arms of a breakwater extending from each peninsula. The breakwater was a wall of giant rocks arching out into the ocean for what seemed like miles. On calm days people would walk out on the breakwater or fish off the sides careful to avoid the colored floats that marked the lobster pots below. Other days the ocean would rain a spray of seawater on the rocks feeding the barnacle-covered lower ones with algae.

We made slow process into the harbor as the channel markers stretched and widened. To my surprise Ed took us straight out of the harbor into the open Atlantic. He said with the prevailing tides and currents we could drift fish for flounder while being carried back towards the harbor. Ed steered us out farther to his projected starting point for the drift as I cut strips of frozen squid and baited the hooks of two short boat rods. We cut the engine and lowered the long weighted lines down to the bottom, then brought them up a foot or two. We sat on old yellow square life preservers to cushion the wooden benches. We bobbed up and down as the skiff rose and fell over Atlantic rollers. I would occasionally have to bail with the cut off plastic gallon bleach bottle provided with the boat, the owner's answer to its obvious slow leak. The breakwater would come slowly into view and grow, until Ed would restart the outboard and head us out for the next drift. As the day progressed the waves intensified and our drifts became more like amusement park rides tipping our silhouettes on the horizon from vertical to nearly prone. We weren't having any luck with the fish and even Ed was a bit concerned about the rising seas. He decided the next drift would be inside the breakwater.

We cut the engine inside the harbor's western edge for a northeasterly drift deeper into the harbor and towards the eastern arm of the breakwater. I was relieved. Waves were now smaller, similar to our first drifts in the open Atlantic. We still had no luck with the flounder as the distance breakwater moved closer. At about fifty yards from the rocks I began reeling in and said, "About time to move?"

"Yeah," Ed replied and began doing the same.

When the lines were in, Ed rose and pulled the starter cord to restart the outboard. "Snap!" The plastic handle was in his hand with two feet of severed cord.

"Oh, no."

This was a mild reaction compared to the panic that raced through my heart. Ed took off the cover to the outboard and retrieved the rest of the cord. The remnant was longer and Ed wound it around the cylinder head, pushing it into the notched channel for the starter cord. He left six inches to grab onto and gave it a pull.

"Prr, prr, prr."

The three revolutions were not enough for the motor to catch. My eyes widened as I looked back to see only twenty yards between us and the rocks that would thresh the boat to pieces as the waves threw us onto them. Ed again threaded the cord around the cylinder, and again with the same result. I could now see the panic in his eyes, though he was reticent to acknowledge it verbally. Ten yards from the rocks and I could see the lobster pot markers jerking themselves upright through the receding waves. I imagined trying to claw up the seaweed and barnacle-laden rock wall as the next wave washed us off. One more pull with half the cord and miraculously the engine caught. We motored away from the breakwater, relief and salt spray washing over us.

I had had enough adventure for one day and Ed reluctantly agreed we should head in since we weren't certain we could restart the motor. After a few deep breaths and the reassuring constant whirl of the outboard, Ed said, "You want to take her in?"

My reaction was mixed due to our close escape in rough seas, but being of an age when a boy wants to drive anything he gets his hands on, I said, "Sure."

We exchanged positions and I grabbed the stick to steer us into the channel. The boat was sluggish, underpowered and now traveling against a strong current. When we hit wakes from the larger boats heading out, the skiff would lift high and the prop would come out of the water producing a deafening whine while losing power and steering. Ed paid no attention to this.

His true intentions were revealed when I saw him drop a line overboard and begin trolling the channel. As I fought to keep course, the Block Island ferry approached and passed. It seemed as if the Empire State building went by leaving two ants in a rowboat in its wake. Ten more minutes of white knuckled navigating and I finally had the skiff into the harbor's no-wake zone where our lack of size and speed were minimized. Moments later, I was a happy sailor to be back on the dock. We didn't speak about our close call on the ride home, and certainly not with Alice.

My last fishing experience happened a few years later. Ed had invited his old boss Charlie out to go perch fishing on Worden Pond in southern Rhode Island. By this point Charlie was quite elderly and had become a bit frail. Ed asked me to come along as an extra set of hands and I was looking for a change of environs, so I agreed. We drove up to Cumberland to retrieve Charlie and then down the west side of Narragansett Bay into South County. Charlie answered the door looking ready to go, his fishing vest and cap worn over a flannel shirt and khakis belted under his armpits. I grabbed his tackle box and rod as he gingerly navigated the walk towards our car. We rented an aluminum boat at Worden Pond that looked pretty good compared to the wooden skiff in Point Judith. We had the 3.5HP outboard again, along with its current and previous owners and gear. Ed was at the helm with Charlie on the center bench and me up in the bow on the short bench. The boat sat a bit low in the water, but all seemed fine. Worden Pond was no Atlantic ocean.

We motored out to the deepest part of the pond, baited hooks with live minnows and started fishing for yellow perch. In minutes Charlie had a bird's nest of line gathered on his reel. Ed set his rod aside and took Charlie's to begin the slow process of untangling the mess. After thirty minutes I could see the frustration in his face and took over the unwinding, letting Ed get back to fishing. He immediately caught the first perch of the day, followed closely by another, and his outlook improved. I had Charlie back fishing and was about to grab my rod when I noticed my feet were wet. In the V of our aluminum hull there was a couple of inches of water and I knew it wasn't splashed in the boat. I found a Styrofoam coffee cup and starting bailing, but it was difficult to collect the water from my position in the bow.

Charlie had another perch on the line and so did Ed. Ed netted each one and in turn slid them onto a nylon stringer floating off the stern. I tried to get in on the action in between stints of bailing, but the bites subsided. We were now all sitting with our feet in ankle deep water. Ed pulled in the stringer and started the motor. We were off to try another spot across the pond. There would be no stringer of fish in the prop today.

We glided to rest in our new position and to my surprise I looked down to see the once captured perch swimming in the bottom of the boat. They had slipped off the stringer during the ride. Ed had his line in the water immediately, but I was torn between trying to re-catch the fish in the bottom of boat and bailing. I started with bailing in an attempt to keep the water at its current level, a process that I repeated for the remainder of the day. Then I turned my focus to re-capturing the fish, but had little luck, as my grabs were futile against the crafty fish cowering beneath the center bench in five inches of water.

I was about to start fishing again when Charlie said; "I think I can get some action with my Rapala swimming lure."

With that, he lifted the top handle of his unlatched tackle box, dumping most of its content into the water in the bottom of the boat.

"Darn!"

I looked down to see the full splendor of our mobile aquarium. We had live fish, rubber worms, brightly colored lures swimming by, along with bobbers, sinkers, leader lines, flies, and jigs. That's when I realized that today my fishing would be restricted to inside the boat. For a moment, I thought my chances of re-catching the perch had risen with all the lures in the water. That image was quickly replaced by a vision of barbed hooks in my fingers. I went back to my coffee cup and began the process of carefully scooping up the tackle box contents, one at a time. Charlie worked with me refilling each compartment, as I turned over freshly retrieved items. He seemed content in re-creating his organizational scheme. After another hour had passed, Ed was willing to cut the outing short, more from a lack of bites than the hijinks with Charlie. As we motored in to shore, I had a sudden affection for the old wooded skiff we took out in the Atlantic. It sure was slow, but so was its leak!

We dropped off a water logged Charlie and went home. We did have perch filets for dinner and the raccoons were happy that night. Up in my room, I pulled off my wet sneakers and socks and looked down at my white puckered feet. I knew I had made my last voyage. I was officially retired from fishing.

· · · · ·

A customer of Ed's at the bank owned a miniature golf course and driving range in nearby Seekonk. He would occasionally leave a handful of free passes with my father when doing his banking. Always in search of some cheap entertainment, I jumped at the chance to go over with Ed and Karen for a game of mini-golf. After several visits during the same summer I decided to try my hand at the driving range. Ed was patient with me as I hit a small bucket of balls after mini-golf. He tried a few but had no real interest, as was the case with most of his sports endeavors. The next season I made a habit out of always hitting a small bucket after mini-golf and started getting the hang of it enough to send my best drives nearly 200 yards.

Later that year a friend from school, Greg, invited me out to play golf on a real golf course. It was a nine-hole municipal course in the woods of Swansea, Massachusetts, and I was allowed to use his mother's old set of clubs. His mother gave us a ride to the course and we unloaded the clubs from the trunk. Greg was using a mixed set made from discarded clubs of his father's and others acquired from garage sales. My ladies' loaner set came with a strange bag/cart combination. It was a rolling red faux leather box sectioned off to allow each club to ride handle up. I guess someone thought making a set of clubs look like a shopping cart would be popular with the ladies. I shrugged off the embarrassment, anxious to see the course and hit shots and putts on real grass. We probably enjoyed the walk in the woods more than the golf itself. Greg stopped at every pond to try to catch a frog or turtle. I liked getting out of the neighborhood seeing each hole's manicured vista and the solitude of the woods. That afternoon was enough to send me hunting for garage sale bargains of my own.

The next time out we were accompanied by Greg's father and played another nearby nine-hole municipal course called Wampanoag. Flatter and less scenic than our first venue, the Wampanoag golf course was bordered on four holes by a salt inlet. The brackish water created a foul smell at low tide. At high tide these same holes became spongy and muddy giving the course its widely known nickname, "Swampanoag."

Greg's dad gave us a swing tips, and some encouragement when we hit the occasional good shot. His father had a short athletic swing that created a penetrating trajectory on his shots. He matched that with a good chipping technique and solid putting to produce an even par score of 36 on the nine holes. Greg and I were both awed by his shot making and scoring. Even though this was by no means a difficult course, shooting par on any golf course requires great skill. What I noticed was the amount of calm and patience he applied when his shots found unexpected trouble. Greg and I both had bad tempers and found it almost impossible to get through nine holes without swearing or throwing a club. I knew his dad normally had the same temperament, but seemed to relax that day on the golf course.

We would get a ride over or drive ourselves to Wampanoag before 8:30 a.m. on Saturdays and take advantage of the special rate $2.50 rate, which meant we could go around the nine hole loop as many times as we liked and still have money for a sandwich from the grill in the little old clubhouse.

I started to build a set of new clubs by purchasing one club with my weekly grocery store paycheck. I would buy a Northwestern brand odd numbered iron from the barrel of loose clubs in the department store, eventually carrying a new 3, 5, 7, 9, and wedge along with my second hand driver and putter. It was during these endless rounds that we found some technique. Greg developed some control and consistency in his iron play and I found power and scoring ability but in a very erratic manner. One day, playing the longest hole a 450-yard par 5, I drove the ball 300 yards and hit a 7 iron onto the green! Why I couldn't repeat it for the entire summer had something to do with inexperience, but mainly my Maditude got in the way. After a bad shot, or a good one with a bad result, I would grip the club like a vice and thrash madly at the ball trying to punish it for its prior sins.

Greg's dad Pete managed to avoid the anger in order to produce a great score that day, even though he had a temper that matched or exceeded ours. He sold aluminum products, doors, windows, and traveled by car covering a part of southeastern New England. He kept his golf clubs in the trunk and would try to find time to use them during the week. At the end of a week of long drives in Connecticut he would be angry as a bear awoken from a long slumber. More than once, he told me to go home because I was hanging around their house too much, avoiding the usual atmosphere of mine.

Pete relied on a CB radio to avoid traffic snarls that could lengthen his day and make him late to sales calls. His house and yard were always immaculate. It was said that if you ever needed to borrow a tool, ask Pete, he has two. If a house repair needed a 2x4 for support, Pete would use a 2x6, always creating the maximum sturdiness. He could not be persuaded against this approach and if you tried, you may encounter the bear's rising temper. When Pete took possession of his new company car, it was with these mental specifications that he began installing the CB radio. First he mated the radio to an oversized steel bracket with enough screws so that no thief could possibly uncouple the pair. He then planned to mount the radio and bracket to the floor of the car. There was a convenient large hump between the driver and passenger seats he deemed ideal. He positioned the brace and drove six large lag bolts into the feet of the brace with a power drill, three on each side. He sat back and gleamed at his work; nobody would be taking that radio out of his new car. After the tools were put away, he started the car to pull it from the driveway into the garage. When he shifted into drive there was a metallic sound and a thud. The car would not move. That convenient mounting hump turned out to contain the transmission, which did not operate well with six lag bolts drilled into it. Pete would have some explaining to do at the office. Making sure we were out of earshot of Pete, Greg and I laughed for what seemed like hours. Yet it was Pete that could go to a different place mentally on the golf course and shoot some great scores. Maybe there was hope for me.

Golf was not a popular sport amongst young people in the 1970s and '80s. It seemed to hold some attraction with older generations and with the wealthy in the country clubs of Rhode Island. For me it was a challenge, but it also helped me with a vision of what life might be like in the future. It was like going to a Providence College basketball game and watching the people enjoy the camaraderie afterwards over a beer at the pub. I liked the Pete that showed up on the golf course and am forever grateful to him for introducing me to the game and how it can be played well.

# '66 Buick

After breaking from the Dumb and Dumber boys and losing my friend Stephen in the process, I'd become defiantly independent. I'm going to do what I want, and I am going to do it my own way, the wrong way. No one is going to tell me anything different. That sums up the complete wisdom of my Plan B. I may bump up against some authority figures like the police, the Catholic Church, and school administrators, but sometimes it's just roadside obstacles that help you reconsider and add to your life's list of what not to do. I was pointed in the wrong direction. This time I was in a car instead on a bike, but still opposing the flow of traffic.

At home, there was some mild curiosity about why the phone didn't ring for "Stoz," my alter ego on the street. Alice eventually asked why I wasn't hanging out with Stephen and was given nothing more than a monosyllabic grunt in return. In fact, I basically gave up talking all together and did not start a conversation for at least a month. I was trying to conjure up some vision of the future. The only current knowns were the thirty hours a week at the grocery store. If I could work in some additional distractions during the week, I might get through a long summer. My lack of social grace and conversation was a combination of anger and disdain towards my current surroundings and prospects. I wouldn't agree with anyone I came into contact with, but was not willing to argue about it either. I'd just stare for a moment and walk away. You couldn't get me to care about the outcome. It was an attitude of being mad without relating it to anyone or anything in particular. I had Maditude.

My musical tastes turned towards punk and new wave with hours spent listening to The Talking Heads, The Clash, Elvis Costello, and The Pretenders, bands that seem to share my Maditude. I also added new favorite films to my list including *Marathon Man* and *Three Days of the Condor*. Both of these films featured individuals in hostile surroundings and circumstances, left with only their intelligence to figure out how to survive. The main characters are flawed. Dustin Hoffman's marathoner is socially inept and haunted by his father's suicide. Robert Redford's researcher is frayed and frightened as he abducts Fay Dunaway at gunpoint only to find a quiet place to think and figure things out. Neither conjures up any super powers or sudden heroics to overcome their plights. They escape by applying their intelligence with a bit of realistic grit. Only with a bit of luck do they survive. I watched these two films in the theater and every time they were broadcast on television, including being featured on *The Movie Loft*. Robert Redford's despair in trying to figure out what was going on around him, filmed against the backdrop of almost colorless gloomy winter scenes in New York and Washington, matched my mood. Their eventual resourcefulness was something I could hope to discover, and the sooner the better.

My first foray with different neighborhood schoolmates had resulted in police arrests that were mainly my fault. I had connected E.T. with Greg, as both were independently my friends. I was the one who bragged about being able to unlock a car in the neighborhood, and the one with the giant bottle of champagne in the backseat.

Our plan was to meet later that night. E.T. could smuggle some beers out of his father's refrigerator, Greg would bring a coat hanger, and I would make it into a tool that could slide through the rubber gasket around the car rear window and grab the top of the button to unlock the door. I claimed to be able to do this in less than ten seconds and the bottle would be ours. I grabbed a pair of pliers hanging with the few tools Ed kept inside the door to the basement stairs, and headed out the next night. We found a spot in the nearby woods to drink the beers and I cut the coat hanger and bent it into a handle followed by two ninety degree turns and a straight run down to a loop. After a couple of more beers each we backtracked to the Dodge Dart and verified the bottle was still on the floor of the back seat. I went to work and in a virtual instance had the button lifted. Greg opened the door and grabbed the bottle. We quickly walked away and found a spot to uncork it. We wandered the neighborhood passing the bottle back and forth until we emptied it. Later that evening, feeling more than relaxed and stupidly basking in the glow of a nearby streetlight, I peered into the darkened rear window of a Oldsmobile Cutlass parked at the end of a driveway. As we continued past the house, I said, "Hey, I think I saw something in the back seat."

The tinted glass had made it impossible to see anything, but my claim was enough to get my new mates to follow me in a loud, clumsy U-turn back to the driveway of interest. E.T. was looking in the driver's side window, I had my nose pressed to the opposite window on the side of the car closer to the house, and Greg was standing near the rear of the car, when we heard the aluminum front screen door snap open, spilling out three armed men.

"Don't move!"

In a single glance E.T. was clamoring over the 8-foot high stockade fence into their backyard. Greg was a flash as he sprinted straight down the street three hundred yards and into his house. They were both good athletes, E.T. on skates and Greg on the soccer field. I was glad to see it put to good use. I was much nearer the hunting party and quickly surmised my efforts would have to be concentrated on not getting shot. I raised my hands slowly and drew all three of them into a tight circle around me.

"Shut up and get on the ground!"

The cold metal of the riffle barrel was jabbed into my back as I was on the ground. I was hoping they didn't have an idea to shoot me in mock self-defense. Sirens sounded and quickly intensified drawing nearer to the house. The eldest man told one of the younger ones to put the guns in the house and not to tell the police about them. Car doors slammed and heavy footsteps shook the driveway.

"We got one of them right here."

"Hands on your head, spread your legs!"

I was patted down, cuffed, and then yanked to my feet by the handcuffs. I was led over to the squad car and tossed into the cage in back. I struggled to sit upright only to see the eyeballs of neighbors from the doors and windows of the surrounding houses. I was suddenly sober. After a few moments I saw E.T. being led across the lawn in handcuffs to the second of the three squad cars now on the scene. Four of the cops were standing together talking. Two others were talking with the older rifleman, presumably the car owner. I realized what we were doing was illegal, but the scene was reminiscent of suspects captured straight from the Most Wanted posters in the post office. Were the cops discussing the reward money with Wyatt Earp over there? I chalked it up to bored cops looking for action on a Saturday night, but there were usually plenty of criminals in the city to keep them busy.

Two of the four cops headed back towards the car I was in. This is where I began to understand that they were used to dealing with heavy criminal element in the city. The first one opened the rear door and ducked down into the backseat. The second one quickly stood behind him blocking the view into the open door from onlookers. The cop lunged at me jamming his forearm across my throat and pinning me down against the seat. With his free hand un-holstered a long metal flashlight plunging the butt end under my ribcage. Pain seared through my chest as the manacles dug into my pinned wrists.

"Fuck!"

"Where's your buddy?"

I struggled to speak with no air to draw from.

"In the other car."

"Wrong answer!"

Wrong answer? That was the technically the right answer. I saw them put him in the car. This guy must not understand how smart I am. Wow, these guys aren't kidding around. I always heard that they knew where to hit you so it didn't leave marks. Do they think I'm Al Capone?

"Where's your friend?"

I hesitated for a moment and then came the flashlight again. This time with a bigger wind-up and a twist at the end that made me think it was in the back of my throat. Fire raced across my torso and into my head. I had to concentrate just to get something out.

"End of the street."

Yup, Greg's house was at the end of the street, right on the way to the police station. I felt shitty about it, but at least he didn't have to make the ride down in a squad car. And by the way, what kind of trouble were we in? Suddenly it's *Dog Day Afternoon* out here. My uniformed friends and I had a pleasant ride to the station as they used every synonym for "scum" they could think of followed by, "Shut the fuck up." Luckily they exhausted their limited vocabulary quickly and reverted to throwing trash through the cage at me while they drove.

So, why were the cops so aggressive with a couple of drunken teenagers? It seems Wyatt Earp and the boys called in a real live home invasion with possible armed suspects. The cops were expecting much more than rounding up a few wayward teens. I would be upset seeing teenagers nosing around my car on the street, looking for something to take, but it was absurd to launch an armed assault and call in the cavalry, when flicking on the porch light would have done the trick. I guess they also thought it was a slow night that needed some excitement. We were very wrong in this situation, but a key lesson was learned. Though not the one you're thinking of. My take away was if you put yourself on the wrong side things, people would relish the opportunity to stick it to you. Everyone involved in this misadventure was disappointed. Wyatt Earp didn't get to shoot anybody. The cop's big collar turned into underage drinking and petty theft through corroboration in separate interrogations. I was disappointed in getting caught by such morons and not being able to avoid Ed and Alice being called to the police station. Ed and Alice were disappointed and embarrassed that they had unknowingly raised John Dillinger. They couldn't understand why I would do such a thing. Ed surmised it was about "getting my kicks," something I had heard once in a Frankie Avalon beach movie from 1960. Alice said I would really be in trouble if they thought I was drinking. So they're shocked that I possessed the sinister criminal mind to plan such a caper but were willing to accept the fact, but can't believe I was drinking? I reverted back to pleading the fifth, not knowing how to possibly explain a lapse in judgment without including the alcohol affecting it.

So there I am in my darkened room upstairs after working the evening shift at Almacs. I'm definitely in despair regarding my immediate situation and I'm in need of some directional change, but I can't quite see it. I'm Robert Redford, minus the looks and Faye Dunaway, holed up trying to figure things out and come up with a new plan. To create Plan B, a plan for my imaginary future, I need a review session on what I have learned up to this point. A mental chalkboard stored my personal life lessons:

1. Whiskey and Tom Collins is a lousy drink.
2. "Gifted" isn't a club you want to join.
3. Fighting doesn't feel that good whether you win or lose.
4. Don't drop an F-Bomb when talking with your teachers. They are easily offended.
5. Stay away from the Mob.
6. Avoid the police.
7. There is nothing wrong with going to church, you might even meet a few girls, but it doesn't make you a better person.
8. People behave differently when money is involved.
9. My ten-dollar bill probably never made it into lost and found at the grocery store.
10. I was falsely accused in the Great French Fry finance robbery.
11. Work involves people, which means hassles, but comes with a check.

12. It's easier to be bossed around when you like what you're doing.

13. Don't look to your parents as role models, the less they know about what you're doing, the better.

I stared at the list like a detective. Was I missing some common thread that tied the list together into an answer? It was going to be difficult to make a plan when you didn't know what you were planning for. What did this future me look like? Where was it that I was trying to find a way to get to? I was back to something I'd learned long ago. You're on your own, figure it out. I didn't have a goal, so I resorted to a few short-term objectives:

1. Sports make life better. Get back into it.

2. Visit naturally beautiful places, they make you feel good.

3. Watch more movies, read more books. Inspire a vision for a different life.

4. Find a way to meet more girls.

So I set out with these motives and the keys to a 1966 Buick Skylark Grand Sport convertible. The same one that Uncle Freddy had crashed into and left the rear quarter panel primer red from a partial repair. It bothered Freddy that we had not done a full repair with a paint job even though he had paid for it. We had bought it as a second car from an older couple living in an apartment complex in town. It had red vinyl bucket seats, power top convertible and windows, and a 445 cubic inch Wildcat V-8 under the hood. It was the woman's car and she cried when we drove it out of the parking lot for $512. When you punched the accelerator the second two barrels of the carburetor would open and the front hood would lift up to match the rising growl of the engine as you lurched forward. You could also see the fuel gauge sink at the same time, which was its largest detriment as we often waited in long gas station lines. Fuel shortages driven by OPEC oil embargos meant you could only buy gas on alternate days based on the ending number on your license plate.

I picked up Greg after work and decided to introduce him to my drive-in movie regiment. Just because I now had a car to drive didn't mean I'd be paying for the movie. We stopped at the package store in Seekonk and hung around out back until we could convince a patron to buy beer for us. Then it was into the empty parking lot of the Ann & Hope store to borrow milk crates and slip through the fence into the drive-in.

We set up in an empty parking space, turned on the speaker, and sat on the crates drinking our beers as the first feature ended. In between movies people were roaming to the concession stand or playground swing set. Three girls we didn't know walked by and started talking with us. I explained that watching the movie out in the open was much cooler than from inside the car. It was certainly cheaper, but I'd hoped I was camouflaging that fact. They seemed reasonable impressed, but eventually wandered towards their car after a few minutes of conversation. We settled in for the second feature by abandoning the crates and using the humped pavement as a recliner, lying against it with our arms folded behind our heads.

The night darkened as the opening credits faded into the gloom of the horror film *The Sentinel*, with a creepy Burgess Meredith. From the darkness appeared the three girls who nonchalantly sat down and then reclined between us creating girl/boy/girl stripes on the pavement. The cutest blond produced a small bottle of brandy that we passed between us in silence as we watched the screen. As the story progressed I had a hard time following the plot due to the interruptions of make out sessions with not only the blond but also the brunette in the middle position.

There seemed to be a competition involved and the stakes were rising as my hands were led to places I always wanted to visit, but wasn't sure I would ever be allowed. This was enough to make a sixteen-year-old boy's brain explode. Greg was getting busy with the tall blond on his end on the line. I not sure how *The Sentinel* ended but our version ended with Greg in the bushes with the tall one and me solely focused on the cute blond, with an angry brunette stomping off. I really wish I had the skills to handle the two-girl equation, especially now that I realize it was an once-in-a-lifetime type of event, but I was lucky to be able to handle the good fortune of one interested girl at that point.

At the end of the night we gathered back at the car and compared enough notes to know we wanted to see these girls again if at all possible. We had their names and knew they went to high school at St. Mary's Bay View Academy, the all girl Catholic school in town. School would be starting in less than a week and we were ready to sign up for some more special tutoring from these not shy Catholic schoolgirls. We made plans to pick them up in the Grand Sport convertible the first nice day after school.

It was a bright Indian summer afternoon with white clouds as high as our spirits, in anticipation of picking up the girls at Bay View. I had been by the Bay View campus hundreds of times growing up, but now the wrought iron fence and gates loomed like a giant chastity belt guarding its entrance. The school was set back a few hundred yards with a single lane drive that circled the stone buildings and spilled back out to the main street. We pulled the Buick in through the open entrance gates, top down, engine purring. As we approached the buildings the drive led us to the right and around back. We closed in on the gothic structures and suddenly we seemed to be on a parade route. Hoots and catcalls snapped our attention to the upper floors where window after window was lined with the waving hands and smiling faces of high school girls. We wondered how long these girls had been locked up in there. We rounded the far corner and started to look for a spot to park until the girls were released from their final period. A loud bell clamored and girls of all ages streamed through the doors like confetti. They filed around the stopped convertible to waiting buses across the parking lot. Out

of nowhere a nun in black habit stormed up to the car like a
mad penguin ready to peck out our eyes:

"What are you doing here!" she screamed.

"We..."

"You can't be here!"

"We..."

"Get this car out of here!"

We were trapped waiting for the girls to clear the
driveway. The background noise of hundreds of girls' footsteps
and chatter at the end of the school day made the scene seem
surreal. The Penguin's rant was continuous depositing spittle
on our frozen shoulders. What had we done to make this bird
so angry? As our pathway cleared, I tried to ask for directions
to the exit drive but her still rising vengeance prevented me
from getting my question answered. At that I resorted to my
old standby:

"Fuck off!"

I squealed the tires and drove up the entrance drive in
the wrong direction to escape to the main road. No girls for us.

Two weeks later, much to my surprise, Ed presented me
with a letter he had received from a local law office. Mother
Superiority Complex had traced my license plate number and

employed her solicitors to send a threatening letter banning the Buick from school grounds for all eternity. Among the list of my sins were speeding, endangering the lives of children, and use of vulgar language. Ed said I was not to use the car for a week, since I seemed to be "living in it."

Not thwarted again by the higher power, we did find a way to meet up with the girls again, but Greg was not all that enthused with his blond in the clear eyes of daytime sobriety. My girl seemed much less interested now that I wasn't proposing something illegal, only just a grope-fest in the park.

Later in the school year I had resumed my basketball career playing for both St. Brendan's and St Mark's Episcopal even though it required attending mass at both. It was a cold February weekday evening, and Greg was riding shotgun again after a close loss at St. Mark's where I had missed the game winner. Roads were plowed but remained packed with snow from several weeks of precipitation.

Nearing home I turned a block early to avoid a stoplight and then again to cut behind the American Legion Hall. Coming out of the second turn I punched the accelerator still thinking about the missed foul line jumper that lost the game.

The Wildcat V-8 lunged forward but unfortunately onto a large ice patch partially hidden by the snow pack on the road.

Without snow tires the engine's torque and power compared to the relatively small vehicle, put us in an immediate fishtail spin. I calmly turned into the spin and began tapping the power brake pedal waiting for the eventual traction that always came. We kept waiting but the combination of speed and ice prevented any change in direction. The only thing that would stop us was the utility pole fast approaching the passenger side. Greg braced his arms against the dash as blood drained from his face. At the last moment the tires found a patch of dry pavement jerking us violently away from the pole and putting us in a reverse spin in the opposite direction. We were now sliding backwards in a reverse fishtail facing the road we had just traveled. We crossed into the empty oncoming travel lane and headed into the snowy sidewalk in reverse. Still carrying a great amount of speed, we skidded diagonally across the front lawn of a house, throwing more snow than a plow, and hitting the rear of a new Lincoln Town Car parked at the top of the driveway. I immediately pulled forward through my snow tracks onto the sidewalk, the Buick now facing opposite of our direction of travel.

I paused for a moment with the thought of driving away, but put the car in park and gathered myself. I realized the house and car belonged to Mr. Saleeba, the voice of Seekonk Speedway. He called the races through the PA system every Saturday night. I nonchalantly strolled to the front door and knocked, truly hoping for no response. This would be the perfect situation to leave a note. The door opened and his eldest son, Tommy, who was my sister Karen's age, appeared. I was about to recount my edited version of a hitting slippery spot and bumping their car when he said:

"You're fucking crazy!"

He had been watching TV in the living room until something more interesting came on in his front picture window, so much for my edited version of events. He disappeared and returned with his parents who spilled out into the driveway in their winter coats and boots. I had one thing on my side. The 1978 Lincoln Town Car may have been the largest vehicle ever produced. It had an enormous four-door cabin flanked by a runway for a front hood and a trunk that could hold eight sets of golf clubs and Jimmy Hoffa. These were encased in matching colored bumpers jutting out eight inches and wrapping around the corners. Mr. Saleeba's flashlight could barely find a scratch on the driver's side rear bumper. With darkness hiding the skid marks across his lawn, and having been spared seeing how I managed to hit his car parked at the top of his driveway, he said:

"No problem, kid, it's just a scratch."

My spirits soared. I had done the right thing and was rewarded with a little luck. I retreated down the darkened driveway with a smile of relief that became an instant grimace the moment I saw the Buick's profile under the streetlight. The front right quarter panel was a crumpled mess. Not wanting to delay my departure, I only hoped the tire would roll freely as I headed to drop Greg at his house. I parked in my usual spot in front of 160 Holland and recounted my adventure to Ed and Alice, leaving out most of the details and focusing on the ice and Mr. Saleeba's kindness. No insurance reports would need to be filed and I would take care of the repair at the Automotive and Auto-Body Repair vocational school attached to our high school.

I convinced a mechanical drawing classmate, who took classes at the vocational school, to use the Buick for an extra credit school project. In the vocational school parking lot I watched as he repeatedly drilled the threaded bit of the dent puller into the folded front quarter panel. As he yanked on the dent puller the metal won the battle keeping most of its concavity. He struggled mightily with this process on several afternoons before giving up entirely. The Buick now looked like it was not only in an accident, but also wounded by a barrage of gunfire. This was how it remained until Ed sold it for $400 the next spring to someone anxious to restore it to its former glory.

In the next few weeks Ed and Alice would come home with a new 1979 Chevy Monte Carlo, probably one of the worst vehicles ever produced by Detroit. On the heels of OPEC oil embargo days, GM made the "Sport" model with a four-cylinder engine that had trouble both starting and passing. It would only be a few short years before Ed would be applying two sided tape to try to prevent the fabric roof liner from hanging on your head as you drove. The "second car" for Ed's weekend fishing trips was now the '72 Dodge Coronet. I quickly went to work on the Coronet replacing the AM radio with a stereo and then adding speakers over a strip of carpeting on the rear window ledge. It would be my primary mode of transportation for the next five years eventually interrupting Ed's fishing. I had had enough fishing to last a lifetime.

# Not a Townie

Even with a head full of Maditude along with my stubborn disposition, I recognized the need for some rehabilitation of my habits. I was going to make some changes but I lacked any real vision of my future. It was an uncomfortable fit at home, in school, or seemly anywhere in the 37 x 48 mile, densely populated plot that is Rhode Island. I yearned for a complete change of venue and looked forward to an imaginary out-of-state college campus filled with coeds in tight sweaters. Instead, I had to finish what felt like my eleventh year of high school.

Back at East Providence High School in the fall I had the feeling of a visitor from another planet. While I was familiar with the dark corridors and location of classrooms, I felt I had little in common with the other 2000 or so students shuffling the halls. Of my potential graduating class of 1100,

I'd guess 25 percent would be heading to college and many less than that if you eliminated Rhode Island Junior College, affectionately known as "Reject." We were the East Providence Townies. Banners at football pep rallies and basketball games declared "Townie Pride!" I wasn't feeling anything like pride. I was focused on the tired city and its less than sunny forecast. But I did not I lack for anything tangible. I had employment, food, shelter, sporting equipment, and transportation. I did not suffer any physical maladies or abuse of any kind. What I lacked was some attachment to the people of my town, school, and home. I was fond of the many things that made Rhode Island "Rhode Island": I enjoyed the ocean, food, and sporting scene, but I didn't feel a kinship. These people were not "my people." I was aware and observant of others in all sorts of capacities: students, teachers, neighbors, politicians, and businessmen. I read the *Providence Journal* every day, but I still had a very hard time envisioning my future here.

I was noticing some of the quieter kids in my college prep classes. There were a few "A" students with upbeat dispositions that relished the thought of writing college essays and filling out college applications. They could see the end of their days of townie pride, but more importantly had a vision of what was next. They had something more than a vision, a plan that they were executing.

Terry sat in the front row of my chemistry class, contently focused on an open textbook and navigating his way to the class valedictorian he would become. He was not one of the handfuls of wealthier kids from Rumford who dressed in monogram sweaters and jeans purchased to dress down and fit in with the unwashed masses of public high school. He wore his familiar painter's jeans and a threadbare brown crewneck sweater. His plan included a perfect transcript from our failing high school, matched with excellent SAT scores resulting in an Ivy League scholarship. His time here was merely a stop along a route leading to the opportunities available to a serious scholar focused on results. His only hurdle was East Providence High's accreditation scare, now openly discussed in newspapers and among the faculty. Our three years of split sessions and short school days filled with mock study halls, now threatened the validity of the degrees we would receive. Terry's aspirations may have been backsliding down the rank order of Ivy League institutions, but it was not evident in his demeanor. He seemed happy to check off tasks on the way to his objective without a care towards the sports, girls, and daily chatter of the social scene. He went about this business of his with an enviable calmness. He did not need to fully assimilate into life here at East Providence High. He was just a traveler passing through, methodically following a map to a future he envisioned.

I spun my metal chemistry lab stool from Terry and the front of the class back around to the buxom full lipped, class vice president candidate I would talk into dating that fall. My plan was full of loose ends and not very well thought out. My grades had easily returned to A's and B's without much effort. I was working my thirty hours weeks at the grocery store and building my savings account. The previous winter I had started running every day with my friend E.T. We had not missed a single day from February 15th through the summer and start of the school year, moving past our base of four miles to seven or eight.

The first week's gym class meant the mandatory physical fitness test that included a 100-yard dash and a 600-yard run. In my 100-yard dash I was quickly passed by a number of boys, but was able to reel in a few towards the finish. In the 600-yard run, a similar scenario unfolded at the

100-yard mark, but by the first turn I was passing the sprinters. By the second turn onto the backstretch, I was by myself. When I finished past the gym teacher staring at his stopwatch I heard: "Not bad!"

E.T. had run his 600 yards in a different class and we both had times in the 1:30s with his an even faster 1:31. We both received visits from the track coach accompanied by invitations to run on the cross-country team. We discussed the prospect on our afternoon run. E.T. took the stance that now we run when we want and nobody tells us what to do. I would have been of like mind just a few months earlier, but I had this new masterful plan of:

Get back into sports

Visit scenic places

Meet more girls

Watch more movies, read more books

The cross-country team certainly checked the first box, and maybe the second if I counted the golf course at the country club where we practiced and held our home meets. I had no preconceptions about cross-country runners getting girls, but thought it might wash off some of my criminal past along with the new haircut I was sporting. When I found out I could fit in the afternoon practices in between school and the start of the weekday evening shifts at the grocery store, I was in.

I asked the store manager to schedule my weekday shifts to start at 5 p.m., which he reluctantly did. I started my running season with practices where I struggled to keep up with the four or five best runners on the team, but easily outpaced my younger and less experienced teammates. I would need to work hard to improve and become a factor in scoring during meets. In cross-country scoring, the top five runner's times on each team were combined to determine the meet outcomes. Our team was captained by Joe, a fun loving senior and hockey player, who was also a scratch handicap golfer and captain of the school golf team in the spring. Joe had no illusions of our team being a powerhouse and said his own times were actually faster when he was a sophomore. This was evident in the first meet of the year when Joe advised:

"Go all out on the opening sprint across the fields."

"I'll be all used up halfway through the race." I said.

"Yeah, but they take a photo for *The Journal* just before we get to the woods."

Sure enough, Joe's grimaced smile appeared along with two others on the back page of the sports section with a caption including his name.

My times improved over the first half of the season, but my biggest problem became getting time off for weekday dual meets. The larger multi-school events were usually Saturday mornings when I could work a full afternoon and evening shift at the grocery store. The weekday meets were in the late afternoon and made working impossible. I did not have a track schedule for the season to try to pre-arrange my work schedule. My manager at the store knew about my track team activity because I had asked for the 5 p.m. shifts for the fall season. Now when a conflict arose in my work schedule, he was reluctant to approve my trading of days with co-workers to accommodate track. My reaction was to call in sick a couple of times to attend the dual meets. During my next shift at work I was called into the manager's office where much screaming, yelling, and threatening occurred.

I had to keep the job for college savings and began to miss meets and practices the second half of the season. My coach would see me in the halls at school and sarcastically ask if I would run again this season. I had no snappy comeback and

I could feel my Maditude taking over. I wanted to tell the store manager off, but found myself in the familiar position of biding my time in the present with some vague idea of a different future. I was mad at myself for letting other people push me around.

The cross-country season came to an end with the State meet held at the rural campus of Bryant College, forty-five minutes northwest of Providence near the Massachusetts border. The course had the usual open field sprint start and finish, but unknown to me, the bulk of the race would be routed through the woods surrounding the campus. I had never run a race in a true cross-country setting because the competing high schools in our division were in larger cities.

It was a more than brisk late fall day as we jogged and stretched in our sweats prior to the start of the race. The wind was cold enough to start a coughing spell after a few pre-race sprints. I decided to start easy and build speed during the race to acclimate to the course and the weather. As the mass of bodies broke from the standing start lined across the width of the athletic fields, I calmly settled into the middle of the pack. The two hundred or so runners formed an ever-lengthening wedge as the stampede approached the woods.

Orange tape marked the opening of the trail we were routed onto. Once the largest part of the pack, including myself, reached the woods, I realized what I had done. The trail was narrow and made passing a difficult and energy sapping exercise. I managed a few passes and avoided fallen runners, one of them a teammate. I was generally trapped in position for the entire two miles of woods. This course routing would leave only 600 yards of open field running to the ending chutes, where you got your ticket with your finish number. Add the five lowest numbers on your team and you had your school score. I finally saw some sun peering through the trees marking the end of the wooded trail. As I exited into the open acreage, an official yelled out our number relative to the field: "119!" I felt panic rising in my throat. Never known as fleet footed in an all out sprint, I needed all of my speed to avoid embarrassment. A long string of runners was spread out across the fields to a turn-around point directing them onto the soccer field for the final sprint to the chute. As I passed tired and slowing runners I began counting, 118, 117, 116. At the turn-around I reached 107, but now in the final 150 yards the runners could see the end and they were giving it their all. I passed three more, then another two. I was in the beginning of the chute and passed the final two. I was now shoulder to shoulder with a runner as the chute narrowed to a single width to determine the final placement. I was spent, but managed to elbow my way in front to grab the ticket with "99" printed on it. I looked over to see the runner holding the "100" ticket and looking back at me was the new women's state cross-country champion. Her face said it all, "What an asshole." She should have been celebrating her win, but needed a minute to see who the jerk was that threw her an elbow at the end of the chute. My finishing 99th in the State meant nothing to the team. It didn't figure into the team score, and we still finished poorly. My impact on the team for the season was much the same.

After the season, my cross-country coach introduced me to the swim team coach saying my fitness and body type might equate well in the pool. My buddy Greg was an all-state high school swimmer and I had experimented the previous summer, going to a training session at the Barrington YMCA run for elite swimmers by a coach that happened to live in the neighborhood. After a week where the warm-up swims were exhausting and 15-year-old girls would fly past me in my "slow lane" assignment, I waved a chlorine fog-induced white flag and quit the offseason training program. And why would my cross-country coach be talking to the swim coach about me? I played basketball in the winter season.

As usual, they knew more than I did as I was unceremoniously cut at the end of basketball tryouts, leaving my teammates to carry on with a couple of awkward sophomores and two empty spots reserved for football players tied up in the playoffs. The basketball coach was implementing a new system of full court pressing and defense to try to keep the under-talented squad competitive in the large school division. It didn't work.

On the home front things were relatively calm. Ed was approaching his 30th year of service at the bank and manned his usual corner teller station on the first floor of the main branch in Providence. Karen was away at school. Alice had her intermittent episodes of crisis with fellow employees, neighbors, and family members, only to be relieved by time and tranquilizers. Her fits of depression hung like storm clouds around the house. Her view that our life was an incredible burden, mostly borne by her, made it hard to feel more than an unwelcome houseguest. I had tried a new strategy of circumventing her list of standard complaints by cleaning the house after school on Fridays. In a complete surprise she would arrive home from work to find the entire house picked up, vacuumed, dusted, both bathrooms cleaned, and beds made. I could manage this in a couple of hours in our six-room Cape. I envisioned a blissfully calm weekend where I would be watching sporting events on the larger TV in the living room. This worked in part as her mood brightened on Friday evenings, but rarely survived the entire weekend.

One week at the Friday night dinner table, she started complaining about all the laundry and ironing she would have to do on the weekend. I looked over her shoulder at the sparkling clean house and wanted to throw my plate at her. Having one extra person in her house could not be this burdensome. Was I was truly the last roadblock to their happy retirement?

Earlier that fall I was surprised when they returned home from shopping on a Saturday and called me away from watching a playoff baseball game to come look in the driveway. They had just bought a new 1979 Chevy Monte Carlo, Sport model. It gleamed in light blue with aggressive looking sporty wheels and tires. New cars did not appear frequently in our neighborhood and there was a certain pride in having such a vehicle in the driveway. I didn't have any idea of the household money situation, other than it was usually very tight. I thought there must have been a breakthrough on that front, since they both preached about never borrowing money on credit; they always paid cash. They used one credit card between them, a MasterCard. They paid off the modest sums they reluctantly charged each month. The twelve thousand dollar 15-year, bank employee rate, mortgage on the house was in its last year. My mind quickly moved on to my own transportation, being unexpectedly upgraded to the 1972 Dodge Coronet, which I loved.

In my mind, I was planning my escape to an out of town college campus and a chance to hit the restart button on life. I was a National Honor Society recipient thanks to my junior and senior year grades and had scored a reasonable 1100 on the SATs the previous spring. I had managed this with hardly taking a book home from our barely accredited high school. Paired with extracurricular activities including an unsuccessful sprinkling of athletics mixed with employment for college savings, I was a less than distinguished college applicant. I stuck with my Oscar Madison *Odd Couple* rerun-driven idea of a sports reporter and dragged Ed and Alice to the

Syracuse University information presentation at the local Ramada Inn banquet room.

Syracuse had one of the best journalism programs in the country and the five hour drive into upstate New York seemed like a great fit. I might even get a serious look as an out of state applicant. At the end of the information session the representatives covered the cost of attending Syracuse and the estimated $8,000 a year including tuition, room and board. On the way out of the Ramada, with information packets in hand, Alice said, "That's a lot of money! You can't afford that."

I waited until we got into the car to bring up my counter arguments, including my $5,500 savings account and the chance to get financial aid. I said I could keep working and get student loans to make up the balance. Well, the mention of student loans set off a chorus of negative comments from the front seat, "You can't go into debt. You'll start off in a hole you'll never get out of!"

What I began to realize was my parent's vision of college was a vocational certification limited to institutions defined by my ability to pay. Financially they were extremely risk-averse, I guessed based on a lukewarm confidence in my ability to achieve at a level that would secure a solid monetary future. I must have looked like a bad bet. But wasn't I the one betting? This argument was repeated on several occasions as I considered additional college choices. They pledged no financial help, and were not willing to help me secure student loans.

The fall of a high school senior is filled with angst about future plans and deadlines for college applications. My friend Greg had applied at a handful of smaller private schools including Babson, Bowdoin, and Colby. All were excellent institutions but came with large price tags. Greg's dad Pete had attended Colby in Maine, which I learned was an advantage for offspring in gaining acceptance. Greg was planning on majoring in business and his application essays revolved around that fact. He was accepted at Babson and eventually Colby, but did not make the cut at Bowdoin. What probably held him back was that his handwritten essay accompanying his application had a spelling error. Long after the postman stamped it, Greg realized he had described his natural inclination towards "buisness" studies and their fine "buisness" school. He was dedicated to the study of business, just not in the traditional spelling. He guessed he had used the word two dozen times in his essay.

The fall school year also meant a mandatory meeting with a guidance counselor. This was my only interaction with her and my Maditude had it written off as a waste of time. Ms. Goggin waved me into her office and I took a seat across from her desk. She asked me about college plans and I mentioned my new target school, Boston College. I think it was $500 less a year than at Syracuse, or so I could argue at home. I told her I had also applied to Babson. This was really a copycat idea from Greg whose future prospects I was beginning to envy. I had no ability to pay for Babson, and ended up on their wait list. Ms. Goggin suggested I include Bryant College where I had run in the state cross-country finals. She talked about the high quality business education available there, along similar lines to Babson, but with more affordable in-state tuition. As usual, I couldn't distinguish good advice from bad and ignored the idea as staying local and becoming a townie.

Ms. Goggin stood as I left and I was surprised to see she was an inch taller than my six-foot frame. Athletically built, she coached the women's tennis team and the men's golf team. She was from Barrington and was a former women's state amateur golf champion playing out of Rhode Island Country Club. In our discussions I told her I played golf and she invited me to spring tryouts and asked if I knew any others since the team was a bit short this year. I made note to mention it to Greg. At home I begrudgingly agreed to apply to the University of Rhode Island (URI), as in what Alice described as a back-up plan.

The next hurdle in my college plan was the alumni interview required as part of the Boston College admissions process. One weekday evening, dressed in my best Levi cords and a crewneck sweater, I rang the Rumford doorbell of my local Boston College alumni. He was a serious man, spectacled in a blazer with elbow patches. We discussed my application and essay on what drove me to apply to B.C. I was never comfortable in his den or with the interview process and my commentary relied mostly on the diligent hard work, and saving to be able to attend B.C. He seemed to have no interest in this. I exhausted the short list of my other accomplishments and began to think about a girl from Rumford and how I had unsnapped her bra strap while making out in the movie theater around the corner. I wondered if she too owned a blazer with elbow patches. I was completely out of my element and it showed. I had no training in polite small talk or self-promotion.

I felt like I was being sent back to the other side of the tracks when he mercifully concluded with, "I guess that's it then."

Greg and I marked the calendar and on an early spring afternoon we drove over to the Metacomet Country Club for golf tryouts. It was a Donald Ross-designed course with the entrance and clubhouse perched atop a steep hill on the Veterans Memorial Parkway leading to the city of Providence. I was familiar with the hill because we sprinted up it repeatedly as one of the workouts on the cross-country team. I couldn't believe we got to play at a private club. It was the main reason Greg and I were trying out. If we made the team we would have a chance to play some of the nicer private courses in the state that hosted local high school golf.

Ms. Goggin stood near the first tee, situated by the clubhouse on the high point of the property. She was talking with a group of people I guessed to be members, maybe including the assistant golf professionals. It was a sunny day and reasonably mild for early spring. I could see members lunching through the wide windows of the low slung, bright white clubhouse overlooking the first hole. Above tables adorned with white tablecloths and sparkling crystal, there were blazers and ties, and pearls resting on lace trimmed necklines. Eight or nine of us stood off to the side of the tee box with golf bags at our sides until Ms. Goggin motioned we could start teeing off. Golf was not a popular sport at any level at this time in the country and you could tell by looking at the mismatched clubs and clothing of our little group of invitees. The first player stepped onto the tee in sneakers, baggy pants bunched into makeshift cuffs, and a hooded sweatshirt hiding his mop of hair. He teed a ball up and unleashed a swing that might have split firewood. The ball jumped straight sideways by the flinching shoulders of Ms. Goggin and crew. The screaming line drive made an echoing boom on the clubhouse siding near the glass of a large paned window. I saw a couple of blue-haired ladies spit out their soup. I was starting to laugh when I saw the look in Ms. Goggin's face. She was angry and with a pointed finger at the end of her raised arm she dismissed the kid from the course. It turned out he was not an invitee, but an interloper taking advantage of the open tryout. I approached the tee next, as some of the red was draining from her face. My soaring drive down the middle was a salve to her wounded pride. I think I made the team right then and there.

Greg joined me as we played down the steep hill of the first hole and then on to the Par 5 second hole that played along an inlet of the bay. The entire length of this crescent-shaped hole was bordered by the bay on the right and was completely visible from the parkway. The inlet waters creped in and receded under the causeway with the changing tides. In the distance you could see tanker traffic in Narragansett Bay approaching the oil and gas depots. We were situated directly between the BP and ARCO depots to our north and south respectively. Oily water lapped against the black mud during hide tide, but at low tide you had to have your car windows rolled up to avoid the rising putrid stench. Greg and I were both distracted by the sun reflecting off a sea of gleaming white dots sprinkled across the black muddy shoreline. New golf balls! We made a pact to somehow retrieve these irretrievable gems and fill our golf bags. We noted the amount of balls and the tide every time we went to a golf match or drove down the parkway for any reason.

Late that spring we hatched our plan. On a sunny Sunday we approached in the Dodge Coronet. It was late afternoon and the course had seen a high volume of play and the tide was still out leaving the black mud densely freckled with white golf balls. We parked along the roadside and I removed Ed's fishing waders from the truck. Greg put them on, and as we thought, they covered his shorter legs right up to his hips. We could avoid trespassing by approaching from the road along the shoreline. Greg would wade into the mud using an extended ball retriever and swing it back to my awaiting bucket at the water's edge. Our only risk was gauging the depth of the mud to make sure he could get back to the shoreline. It was a dirty job but someone had to do it. We methodically erased the white dots from the ash-colored landscape starting with the weaker golf shots and progressing to the stronger players' misses.

If Greg stayed in one spot too long he had trouble extricating his feet from the holes in the mud. As our bucket filled we became more brazen and greedy. Greg waded further from shore to reach the outliers and his next step was hip high in black mud. Knee high mud covered my boots and jeans as I stepped in to help pull him out by the aluminum ball retriever. He struggled to wiggle his leg loose and turn his body back towards the shore. In a fit of maximum effort, he pulled with his arms and free leg in a swimmer's motion across the mud. He was making progress now and our panic turned to laughter.

Back by the car I surveyed the results. A bucket of dirty new golf balls, but the foul-smelling mud was oozing from inside the top of Greg's waders. My original plan was to put the waders back in the trunk and hose them off in the backyard, returning them to their place among the fishing gear in the basement. Now through tears of laughter we concluded that the only way this could work was to have Greg get in the trunk with the waders on. He climbed in and we did a short test with the trunk closed to make sure he could breathe okay. I drove off and was amazed how clearly we could hear each other as I checked on him during the drive. I thought about what an uneasy feeling it must be to have someone tied up and gagged in the trunk like the local mobsters might. I sprayed Greg with the backyard hose and delivered a wet but grateful buddy, with a bucket of new golf balls, back to his house. He could sort and split our loot after a shower and some dry clothes.

That summer we returned to rounds of golf at "Swampanoag" and our other nine-hole cow pastures, but with new Titleist golf balls from the hallowed fairways of Metacomet Country Club!

# Absolute Power

At this point I was doing a poor impression of a clean cut New England preppie. I took to wearing a sweater or golf jacket to high school to avoid being detected as an imposter. I came to realize I lacked power. The social power that helped with admission to better colleges and helped make friends once you got there. And the economic power to pay tuition and allow full immersion into college life while studying. I also lacked brainpower. I was close-minded and angry which restricted my ability to imagine an alternate route to my future. A path would eventually present itself with the help of Aunt Mae, Ms. Goggin, and Greg's father Pete, but not until I found myself headed in the wrong direction again.

My impact on the golf team was similar to my cross-country team body of work. I was unreliable and my efforts bordered on the inconsequential when it came to scoring for the team. In a match against Barrington at the beautiful Rhode Island Country Club, I angered Coach Goggin by tossing my wedge out of a pot bunker on one of the seaside finishing holes. I had climbed down into the sand filled crater in the fairway and taken two swipes to extricate my golf ball. Readying for the climb back out, I threw the sand wedge out first. I was surprised to see she was following my match along with the opposing coach and raced up to me, red-faced, and told me, "Never to do that again!"

My playing time was reduced after that. I thought my club toss was such a mild display compared to what I was capable of. There was no violence in the throw. I didn't swear or hit anybody. I didn't comprehend that I had embarrassed her, at her home club, which was kind enough to host high school golf matches, on a hole visible from the towering clubhouse across the street. We were already beaten that day by a good Barrington team led by future pro Brad Faxon. My mild antics were not welcome in any way.

It took a long time that spring for Boston College to decide to accept me, but they eventually did. Alice's work on the financial aid paperwork had netted a total of $500 per semester in Pell Grants, but nothing more from other sources. We seemed to be in the common middle ground of not being poor enough to qualify for significant financial aid, but we didn't have enough resources to pay for school ourselves. We had already determined I was not gifted scholastically or athletically, which eliminated those avenues for assistance. This probably describes the situation of 99 percent of college students who take out student loans. Since Ed and Alice were dead set against student loans, there would be no co-signing of loan paperwork. That left my backup plan of URI as the only plan, since I could pay for the entire first year's tuition, room and board, and incidentals from my savings.

My Maditude was in full bloom for a month or two as I tried to ignore my classmates' announcements of their future college plans. I didn't want to stay local, see some of the same faces from East Providence High School in the fall, and feel like I was underachieving again. When your future suddenly becomes the present and it doesn't quite live up to the notion you had in your head, however vague it may have been, it's disappointing.

The air on the high school campus was full of optimism. The most common message under the 900 or so headshot photos in the Townie Crimson yearbook was "Let the good times roll," borrowed from the popular Cars' song. Kids were happy to be graduating even if moving on to compete for a job in the difficult local economy. After watching *Apocalypse Now* for the fourth time at the local Cineplex and thinking about what kids my age faced just a decade ago in Vietnam, my half-empty cup started looking more like half-full. At least I was going someplace, and that would be a welcome change.

I knew almost nothing about URI other than its campus location and the sorority houses my sister had lived in during her time there. I found out during orientation that students from other New England states could attend at in-state rates, in fields of study that were not offered at their state universities. I met students from this category that were in the Schools of Pharmacy, Engineering, and Oceanography and were focused and excited to be attending URI and some of its highly regarded academic programs. I could see they were following plans for their future occupations, and I was envious of the certainty in their visions. I, on the other hand, had no plan. I was being released into the sea of 14,000 college students with a major of "undeclared" at a university I had no intention of attending. My academic intentions were unknown, but would be somehow clarified during a year of general studies. I did think it was a great place to meet girls and the athletic facilities were super and open to students at all times of day and night.

I was a bit disappointed walking into my freshman dormitory. I found the same dingy gray, insane asylum floor tiles and painted cinder block of my high school. In my narrow room, stood two small metal beds and worn chests of draws and desks, facing each other like two fighters coming out for the final round of a fight that should have been stopped long ago. There was a men's bathroom at the end hall that ensured the infirmary would be permanently out of stock in anti-fungal cream. I cringed thinking about the $2,500 drained from my savings account, but I was happy to be on my own.

That first day of fall classes I found my way across the large campus to the building for my Political Science 101 class. I stopped and re-checked the room number on the door. I was expecting a classroom and found an auditorium. I found a seat about three quarters of the way up the center section amongst the other 200 students. An older professor entered and stood on the floor below. He scratched "Poly Sci 101" onto the rolling green chalkboard and said, "If that's not your class, you're in the wrong place!"

He turned back to the chalkboard and wrote "POWER." He shouted, "POWER!" and spittle rained down on the first row. He defined it, turned and wrote the definition on the board. It was hard to read the yellow chalked handwriting against the green board from that distance. Could some of my $2,500 go to a projector and maybe a microphone? It was 1980 after all. As the lecture continued we eventually got to the spittle-flying concept that, "Absolute power corrupts absolutely!" What a revelation. Absolute power is what they had. They had my money. I had no power. And this was how I would be getting my educational value.

It was a similar experience in all of my classes. As the semester wore on, the auditoriums would be less and less full. Students would agree to the pass lecture notes between them. Former students of the same teachers would pass along advice as to how much testing was done against lecture notes versus the accompanying textbook. Tests were sometimes as much as 90 percent against a book that was seldom mentioned in lecture hall. When lecture notes were emphasized, you were to regurgitate them back into blue book essays as though they were your own ideas. I could get this education at Providence Public Library for free!

Since my study habits from high school were virtually non-existent, spending most of my time teaching myself new subjects from outrageously priced textbooks wasn't a natural fit. I set my sights on a 3.0, B average, and just missed. I thought this crazy teach yourself method must be a first semester thing they did to freshman, but I was only beginning to find out how things really worked when it came time to register for spring classes.

At my appointed time during the end of the weeklong spring class registration period, I presented my registration slip for admittance in the basketball arena. I arrived and found a long line winding out through the double entrance doors to the court and running down the corridor and past the locker rooms. When I reached the front of the line an hour later, I peered in at what looked like a giant flea market.

Folding tables and chairs were set up in every area of the gymnasium. Banners were taped to the front of tables with the names of the various college departments. If you were interested in taking a course in English, Math, Physics, Speech, History, Business, or anything else, you needed to find that department's table. Once found, you would line up to speak with someone at the table to sign up for a particular class.

That's if you had the proper prerequisites and there was an open section of the class available. Many classes were full and closed, but you could put your name on a list if they were considering opening another section. It usually didn't happen, but there was the chance of an additional class being added to the schedule at an odd time, taught by teaching assistant or adjunct professor with a twisted arm, maybe at night. You could spend hours wandering around trying to put together a schedule of classes.

Some departments had class sections reserved for only those majoring in particular fields. "Undeclared" majors would have better luck rebooking a flight at Logan during a snowstorm, than getting into classes with the better instructors at reasonable hours. The flea market had been picked over for five days, but I was required to buy five items and pay the same price as the first ones in the door. I left with a schedule that included a speech class that I didn't understand the title of, a plant and soil science class, and something called "Political Geography".

This was how I was supposed to discover my true field of interest and possible career? Was I supposed to find something in one of these books that suddenly turned on a light

and pointed me down a path to my future? I felt suckered
again. Why didn't somebody tell me about this scam before?
But if they did, I probably ignored them.

By then end of the spring term I had two Bs, three Cs,
and empty bank account. I had almost gotten the first D of my
life in that speech class. It was an evening class with all older
students except myself, and required public speaking. I was
barely speaking to anyone let alone standing up in front of a
class. I had some vicious Maditude going now, eased only by
the occasional keg party, football game, or other excuse to
drink. Late in the term I brought the '72 Dodge back from
home to move out of the dorm room. Thursday night I drove it
from party to party around campus. I finished the night off at a
grain alcohol frat party. I was sleeping off my big night when I
was awoken by the sound of a car starting. I thought I must
have left my dorm window open because not much could wake
me on a Friday morning. My head screamed and my eyes
struggled to focus. I was disoriented as I stared at the threads of
a bolt and the nut holding a clamp in place. I tried to clear my
head and my eyes moved from the clamp and followed the pipe
it supported. The pipe went through another clamp and then
into a muffler. A muffler! I was under a car! In a panic I

squirmed out from underneath, banging my elbows and knees. I found myself in the South Lot A, not too far from my dorm. Shaken, I hurried back to my room. My watch said 6 a.m.

The following day was Saturday. Move out day. In a much more routine start of the morning I went out to the parking lot to pull my car around to the dorm to load it. I walked up and down the parking lot rows and couldn't find the Dodge. I was stumped. I retraced my Thursday night escapade to other dorms I visited and frat house lots. I was on my way to the campus police station to report it stolen when I spotted it in an alleyway, parked with two tires up on the curb and a windshield full of tickets I couldn't afford. I had apparently abandoned any thought of driving midway through my night of party hopping.

If a college education paves the road to success, why did I feel like I was going the wrong way on a one-way street? I was angry at the world. I had a lead on a summer job, since the grocery store didn't hire back summer help based on the Amalgamated Meat Cutters union rules. The union had guaranteed me incremental pay raises from my starting minimum wage, which made the job somewhat lucrative during my high school years. The new job lead was at private school specializing in kids with emotional and learning disabilities. They hired a couple of college kids to paint and landscape during the summer. The St. Andrews school was near the scene of my bike crash with Stephen, and I felt like I was still riding on the wrong side of the street. I went by early and was hired on at minimum wage.

Every morning I reported to the garage area adjacent to the campus and got my assignment for the day. Mostly we painted and stained the exteriors on campus buildings and on Friday we cut lawns and athletic fields. I was partnered with another college student. He was from Barrington, a year older, and on break from St. Lawrence University, a very good private college in upstate New York. I didn't say much at work or home, but spending every day with someone painting on a parallel ladder, it was hard not to chat a little in between songs on the radio. He was planning to follow his father in his insurance practice and was majoring in business at St. Lawrence. He asked about URI and wondered if I was an engineering major. I said sure. It seemed that I was at the point where I needed to decide on the rest of my life and I wasn't allowed to be "undeclared" as a sophomore. There was one more secret I discovered about URI. If you didn't apply to a specific college within the university initially, you had to apply to transfer into that school after freshman year. Oceanography, Pharmacy, and others did not accept any transfers. The business school required a 3.0 GPA, which I didn't have. The school of Engineering had prerequisites of calculus, physics, and chemistry that if I completed I could transfer in. It seems that I wasn't really in college that first year after all. I did have credits, but I was at a loss as to what to do with them.

I worked 6:30 to 3:30 five days a week and saved every nickel from my paychecks. In the evenings I would go running with E.T. and try to formulate a new plan of attack. I didn't want to go back to URI, but lacked any imaginative alternatives. My hair grew long and was now matched with a scraggly beard. My body thinned out with the running and was darkly tanned from working outside every day. My bank account recovered very slowly and by summer's end had barely over a thousand dollars. I was going to be a thousand dollars short for the fall and had to bring up the topic with Ed and Alice. I thought I'd better take some time off. This set off the usual anxiety at home. I didn't want to go back; they insisted and decided to make up my shortfall. That would lead to quite a predicament in the spring when I would be dead broke.

On my longer runs I thought about ways out. Maybe joining the military would work. Then I thought about my sixth grade teacher, Mr. Travers of the "fucking Toomey" incident. Later in that same spring he had our class out practicing kick ball for our upcoming challenge against another sixth grade class. There were four sixth grade classes, but only two who were close in athletic abilities, and this was the finale as the school year was about to end. When he ordered us to line up to file back into our classroom, several of us asked if we could stay out longer to practice. The opposing class was habitually extending practice time to ready for the match. Mr. Travers reaction was to mock us. He mimicked our preadolescent voices:

"Why can't we stay out longer?"

"Ms. Cochin's class is staying out!"

I thought this was degrading and crossed the line, so I simply replied, "Oh, shut up!"

Mr. Travers face got red and his eyes got big. He stormed back and forth demanding to know who said it. He looked like Mussolini addressing the troops. He was about the same size. He threatened the class with all types of sanctions. I had seen this rage thing enough at home and ended the group problem by stepping forward:

"I did."

There was a rumble of whispers amongst my classmates as they were marched back up to their desks and ordered to sit with folded hands in silence. For me, it was just another session of shirt collar grabbing, threats of parental involvement, and detention. It was the end of the school year. What could he really do about it? And he was wrong, by the way. Maybe this join the military idea I was floating in my head was not such a good one.

I thought about taking the thousand dollars in my account and buying a bus ticket out of town. But without a job, car, or place to sleep it wouldn't last long. Besides, I couldn't get that image out of my head of Dustin Hoffman on the bus in *Midnight Cowboy*. Ratso died on that bus ride. I had no plan again, but I was adding something to my list. Make some fucking money! It was going to the top, ahead of girls, sports, nature, books and movies.

It was with this Maditude, walking directly towards the machine gun fire that I returned to URI in the fall. I had managed to schedule the calculus, physics, and chemistry classes along with a couple of other dogs. This seemed like the proper punishment for not knowing what I was supposed to do with the rest of my life.

I walked into a stone building on the quad and found a second floor classroom. It was an actual classroom with chairs and desks and held no more than fifty students. Maybe I was finally onto something, or was it my sophomore status that had me avoiding the little man in the big auditorium. The professor barely acknowledged our existence and began half-heartedly scratching on the chalkboard. He was both distracted by an imaginary problem he seemed to be working on, and disgusted at the level of simplicity he was descending into in communicating with us. I couldn't read his writing, and then he began speaking in a very thick Indian accent. It was pleasant in a singsong sort of way, but I was missing every other word. He said, pointing to the unreadable board behind him, "You must devil-up vroooom-u-luz, and sub-tea-toot wail-yooz!"

The formula that jumped to mind was how in the hell was I going to teach myself calculus from a textbook, and the values were the zeroes in my bank account! It was much the same problem in my physics and chemistry classes as grad students with poor English skills would try to teach me subjects I had no natural inclination for. This was all in preparation for a career in a field I had no interest in, chosen because it was highly regarded at the university I had never intended to attend. Sound like a good plan? At the end of each day of classes I would return to my dorm room, lock the door, and turn my roommate's stereo up to ten and blast "Hells Bells" by AC/DC. The echoing clang of bells at the beginning of the song had fellow students and the R/A (Resident Assistant) pounding on my locked door. I couldn't really hear them with the music that loud and did not relent until the final chorus of "…you're only young but you're gonna die!"

After some predictably bad mid-term results my mood worsened. My roommate was a friend from high school and a year ahead in engineering studies. He told me that everyone would have bad grades and most of the time the professor would scale them up at the end of the term to create some Bs, Cs, and Ds. So in this system, I would learn barely 50 percent of the material I supposed to, but rely on the random kindness of the instructors to give me passing grades I didn't deserve? And I was paying a lot of money for this.

When final exams came around I wanted to burn down buildings on campus. I loaded up the Dodge and drove back to Riverside. I was penniless and pissed off. The reaction at home was full of consternation and threats that I would have to get a job if I wasn't going back to school. Did they think I only wanted to lounge around in the peaceful confines of Holland Avenue? Of course I needed a job, and some possible scheme to get the hell out of there!

A rage was burning almost visibly beneath my skin. I was extremely anxious about my future and didn't sleep well. Sadness settled in when I began to worry about something different. Isn't this what Alice had done for years? She would become upset with people and the circumstances of her life. She would quit jobs and be difficult to be around. She would incessantly worry and lose sleep, working herself into a state of permanent anxiety. Wasn't I showing the same signs of whatever demons haunted Alice? I made a promise to myself that December. If I had the same problem, I would get out on my own and not bring anyone else down with me. I would stay single, not have a family.

I found a job at the local convenience store. They were expanding their hours and needed someone to open up six days a week at 6 a.m. A friend of my father's from the bank was told about my status and mentioned he knew the dean of admissions at Bryant College. If I sent in an application, they thought I could get in for spring term. I jumped at any chance to move forward and sure enough I was accepted for spring term. There was one big hurdle in front of me. Bryant's tuition alone was as much as tuition, room and board at URI. I was readying myself for a big argument about taking out student loans, when I was awestruck. My Aunt Mae stepped in and said she would pay for my semester. Yes, Aunt Mae and Uncle Jesse where still keeping an eye on Karen and me. They would help Karen by selling her their house as they moved into my grandparent's vacated place, and then return her money when she was ready to buy her future home. For me, I was going to be able to go school that spring.

At Bryant there were some noticeable differences. My classes were easy to schedule and were held in classrooms with no more than thirty students. Professors were present and engaging. There were no teaching assistants standing in for them. Most of the four thousand students were pursuing a bachelor of science in business administration. This degree afforded a concentration in an area of business (i.e. accounting,

Maditude

marketing, etc.), but also required a fair share of sciences and electives to round out your education. Bryant was able to focus on this degree path, and with that focus came excellent quality.

I immediately felt like Aunt Mae's money was being well spent. In that spring semester of mostly business courses, I had a GPA of 3.6. In following semesters, I enjoyed mixing in my elective choices, spent mainly in English, History, and Art History. I also found a natural affinity for Economics. Economics was a mostly required subject through the semester tracks, but one I enjoyed throughout, always adding As into my GPA.

I would work the early shift each day at the store; then drive to campus for classes in the late morning and early afternoon, and spend the remainder of the day in the library. Class sizes were small and I never missed class, because I was learning. I was paying for these professors to teach and they seemed compelled to hold up their end of the bargain. What a concept. Now I just needed a plan to keep it going.

· · · · ·

Greg was home from Babson that January and he was hatching a plan for his summer. A couple upperclassmen he knew had worked at the Lighthouse Inn and Resort on the Cape. One day the previous spring, I had been back out to the Cape golfing with Greg and his dad near their family cottage along the Bass River. Our problem was how to get on the radar screen for jobs that were mostly filled by word of mouth at this family-owned resort. Greg's dad's answer was to call them up early and ask for an interview. We struggled with this idea, doubting that either of us could pull it off successfully. After a week, Greg's dad picked up the phone, raised his voice an octave, and convinced the owners to let us come down for an interview. We went down one snowy Saturday in early February and presented ourselves at the front door of their home. I got a chuckle out of the proprietor's wife looking at my business attire. The same cords and sweater from my alumni interview mismatched with my Herman Survivor work boots. We were genuine in our interest and very early in the application season. At the end of our visit we heard the magic words:

"OK, boys, I'll give you a job this summer."

We were excited during the hour and half ride home and started making plans to find rooms to rent for the upcoming season.

The Lighthouse Inn presented earnest young college men to serve you breakfast and dinner daily during your weeklong stays. We dressed in logoed golf shirts for breakfast and dress shirts and bow ties for dinner, always with black slacks and polished shoes. The uniform was not complete without a nametag that included the college you were attending. You could chat with your server during mealtime or just gaze out the picture windows looking into the Atlantic. It looked like a scene from the movie *Dirty Dancing*.

Greg and I arrived the first week of May for training. Included was basic serving etiquette and a tray-carrying test. We carried large oval brown trays filled with old china out the deck doors, over the lawn, and out to the end of the jetty and back. We would be serving weddings, banquets, and luncheons during the early season and be evaluated for the assignment of serving stations in the dining rooms. There were twelve candidates; half were experienced returning waiters for the ten stations. The two worst performers would be "relish boys" which meant they would serve all the tables in the dining room with jams for breakfast and condiments during dinner. They could count on only a small fraction of the tips. The best stations in the dining rooms had the largest windows and the most ocean view tables. The better the station, the better the clients the maître d' would be seating there. Tables were assigned for the entire stay of a guest and factored in their history and tipping habits compared to the recommended amounts in the resort brochure.

It was a big stretch to think I was going to excel in the social graces and small talk required of a successful waiter, but I had a strong motivation. I needed to maximize my summer income in order to stay in school. There were protests at home when I drove the Dodge off in May to the little cottage bedroom I would share with Greg and a grad student who worked at the Chatham fish pier. It was four hundred dollars each for a season of sleeping on homemade bunks in a cloud of dead fish odor. Ed and Alice complained that I didn't even ask about taking the car. They were right; I was taking the car, nobody got a vote. I considered transportation as part of their support of my college education.

I had a couple of things on my side. I was observant of others and had a memory like an elephant. Both came in handy in learning the ropes and being a good waiter. I was challenged in the social confidence area, but observed others and copied their techniques the best I could. Good balance, hard work, and reliability got me assigned in the second dining room with a handful of tables overlooking the Atlantic. Greg got a station in the first dining room. Smaller windows and a shorter walk meant a proliferation of older guests, but still a good income. We had both made the grade, no relish boys here!

During the wedding and banquet season I made back my rent money quickly. With the Inn filling up for the guest season and some of my prime tables being re-seated for transient off-the-street diners, I had a built-in system of savings. The transients and lunch tips kept me in pocket money. The guests presented a tip envelop at the end of each week's stay that went straight to the bank. My $1.99 wages were kept with the Inn bookkeeper to be disbursed in a single check at the end of the season.

Every Wednesday I was off. The two relish boys rotated in creating an off day for two waiters. Three of the other six days I didn't have to work lunch. I was out by 9:45 a.m. and not back until at 5:15 p.m. for dinner set up. I could drive up to the beaches on the Outer Cape and National Seashore, surf for a half-day and be back in time to serve dinner. At the end of August I had $3700 in my savings account with another $800 coming in wages. That was tuition for both semesters! I still had the fall wedding and banquet season where I could earn a few hundred dollars more while commuting back to college during the week. After this wrapped up on Columbus Day weekend, I would find my way back into the convenience store opening shift, which helped pay for books, food, gas, and rent. I finally had a workable plan.

Cape Cod was full of college students, happy hours, and other things I could deprive myself of during the cold weather months while working the early convenience store shift and studying. When I felt the grind of class work and the accompanying empty bank account blues, I could always think about the upcoming season and smile.

My first season did not come off without a few hiccups. There was the buttery knife that slide off the tray and down the back of a women's gown during a wedding. She reacted as if she had just jumped into an ice cold bath, but then flirted with me about retrieving it. I apologized and smiled, but thought how easy it was to be around happy people at parties or on vacation. There was a good sense of camaraderie among the staff that included Sunday afternoon softball games where the wait staff played against the kitchen crew. I didn't realize it at the time but I was learning social skills and teamwork that would benefit me later on. I also learned some other things about myself, like not to pursue a career in the medical field.

I was running a transient diner's bill up to the hotel desk for credit card processing and walked by open stairway to the lower deck bar. The lower deck was a combination of a lounge and family game room on the first floor looking out from beneath the dining room deck. As I walked by I heard a muffled plea, "Help me, help me..."

I glanced down and saw an older guest lying on the carpeted landing of the stairway, her bright printed dress bunched and twisted. On second look I saw her beehive hairdo had tried to continue on without her. It was bent around the corner of the landing, heading for the second set of stairs. My instinct to assist was immediately overwhelmed by a focus on suppressing laughter. I scurried into the butler's pantry to let out a yowl. I pointed a responsible relish boy in her direction, unable to completely regain my composure. All turned out fine as others rushed to her aid to find her mostly scared. Once up-righted and her railing hand firmly wrapped around a fresh Old Fashioned, she regained her bearings. I wondered what was in an Old Fashioned.

# Songs and Comedy

I'm actually on the upswing now and learning a few things about myself. I'm a hard worker if given some clue about the long-term objective. I may be more suited to the bartending profession than I realized, but I can certainly scratch emergency medical technician off the list. I'm becoming self-sufficient and climbing the economic ladder, but not before slipping on a rung and smashing a jug bottle of white wine. Once I sweep up the glass I'll be rewarded with a chance to meet Ross Perot and start a higher paid adventure.

. . . . .

One summer morning after serving breakfast at the Inn, rain precluding our usual surfing and outdoor activities, we decided to have a party. Greg and I invited co-workers back to our neighborhood rental cottage for Bloody Marys, beers, and a couple of "Cheech and Chong" joints. I sifted through our roommate's album collection to find Buffalo Springfield, Dylan, and The Doors' records as we partied away the rain. The crowd dwindled by lunchtime, then again to just the two of us in the early afternoon. I drove to the grocery store and bought fixings for the two giant cheeseburgers and made them back at the house. Drunk, stoned, and satiated by cheeseburgers our eyes grew heavy. After nodding off in a chair listening to a Rod Stewart's *Every Picture Tells a Story* album, I went back to my bunk for a nap.

"It's six o'clock! It's six o'clock!" Greg screamed trying to rouse me from my face down pillow plant. Groggy, I told him to relax:

"We don't have to be in till 7:15."

"Get the fuck up, we gotta go!" he shouted.

I started to argue and he cut me off:

"It's dinner! It's dinner!!!"

"Shit!" Suddenly I realized it was not morning. I grabbed for my blue dress shirt and black bow tie. I found my keys and raced to the car in the driveway. I sped down the

access road to the Inn while Greg changed his shirt in the
passenger's seat. I screeched to a spot in the parking lot and ran
up the back stairs into the kitchen. Over my shoulder I could
see my guests walking up the stairs to the front dining room
entrance. Once inside the dining room, our panic started to rise.
All my tables were bare with the breakfast condiments
remaining from my quick wipe down that morning. Thom, the
maitre d', was marching towards us with daggers in his eyes.
Thankfully he had closed the wooden accordion doors sealing
off our mess from the arriving diners.

"What the hell's going on here?"

"Sorry, just got here," I replied.

"Get your shit together!"

We frantically set our tables, now with the help of co-
workers who saw the anger in Thom's face. Out front, Thom
delayed the diners another moment then squeezed back through
the doors to check on our readiness. We were half groggy and
half shaken when he found us in the butler's pantry. I was
straightening my tie and we told him we were all set. He
opened the doors and began walking the backlog of guests to
their assigned tables. On one of his trips back to the lobby he
ran into Greg coming out of the kitchen. He was close enough

so Greg could feel the breath on his face as he grunted through his clenched teeth:

"Where are your shoes?"

Flames burned in his pupils as a puzzled Greg looked down to see he was wearing his white high-topped basketball sneakers instead of black dress shoes. Thom scornfully shook his head and motioned Greg into the butler's pantry. He kicked off his own shoes for Greg to wear and then scurried off to retrieve a second pair from his living quarters on the property. Greg and I spent hours shining all the silverware in the restaurant with the burnishing machine one sunny day, but we kept our jobs.

By our third summer we had done a bit of everything at the resort and were promoted to work at the Sand Bar. The Sand Bar was a rustic, low-slung piano bar owned by the proprietors of the Inn, which sat out on the access road to the public beach. Outside it was non-descript with a gravel parking lot abutting a salt marsh and crabbing creek. From a post in the front lawn swung a painted wooden sign announcing "The Songs and Comedy of Rockwell King."

We were excited for a change in work venue but mostly drawn to the idea of $200 in tips on busy nights, weekends and holidays. On those nights patrons would line the flagstone walk out front for a second seating at 11 p.m. Low, nicotine-stained ceilings looked down over forty cabaret tables barely big enough for four or five drinks, some stationed on an old converted porch. To the right of the front door was an alley of overcrowded barstools and bar with a service area on one end facing the piano floor.

The Sand Bar crowd was middle-aged and higher, but could often include multi-generational groups of adult children with their senior citizen parents. It was a hard-drinking, smoking, loud, boisterous crowd, somehow kept orderly by our hostess Mary. Mary manned the door on all of the busiest nights, organizing the crowds for the multiple sessions and handling seating requests. Her weapons of choice included a Virginia Slim in one hand and a "Stinga" in the other. Part of my duties included keeping that Stinger fresh. It's a cocktail of brandy and white crème de menthe shaken with ice, creating effervescent foam spilled into a rocks glass. Mary had Irish features and complexion topped with a permanent, shaped like the beauty parlor hair dryer that created it. Her raspy voice somehow penetrated the bar noise and transformed my first name into a multi-syllabled swimming hole: "Po-o-o-o-l-l-l."

She could tell a racy joke and follow it with an infectious bellowing laugh. Her easy way and warm smile made people feel she was inviting them in to her own party. I loved Mary and the happiness she spread.

Our workday started with bar prep at 7:15 p.m. each evening, and ended at 2:30 a.m. with a quick cleanup after closing. I would be cutting fruit behind the bar when Rock King would arrive on an old bicycle complete with a basket on the front handlebars. I never knew where he came from, but he always arrived ready to perform, in straw hat and bow tie. He was a talented boogie-woogie piano player and sold his albums and tapes during his sets. He had several ballads that were on "the list" behind the bar, meaning we were to desist from running the dishwasher during these songs. The frequent one that stands out in my memory was "In My Room," also the title of one of his albums. Songs were intermixed with jokes he would often tell standing up from behind his piano bench. After hearing his act six nights a week for the entire season, many of us could recite the jokes by heart. One of my co-workers, Marty, could pull off a mean impression of Rock on the piano during our bar set-up time. A joke might involve a plastic phone sitting on the piano with a doorbell button Rock would press to make it ring.

"Ring, Ring!"

"Hello, Doctor Smith, speaking"

In a high-pitched self reply, "Doctor Smith, this is Silvia."

"Yes, Silvia."

"Doctor Smith, did I leave my panties in your office?"

"No, No, Silvia you didn't."

"OK then, I'll check with the dentist."

Rock's act included some intentional slurring of words and jokes featuring drunks that seemed to work well with the general condition of the audience. In the piano microphone he would request a "special" or a "Rock King" from the bar and I would deliver it in between songs. It made the audience feel he was imbibing with them, but the "special" was water with lemon served in an opaque commemorative glass with piano keys around the rim and Rock's likeness stenciled on the side. I wasn't sure whether this was a chance to remind the patrons to buy a glass or a past problem Rock may have had, necessitating his arrival by bicycle each evening. He was not friendly with the staff, with the exception of Mary, and I would occasional return the sentiment with a whirl of the dishwasher during "In My Room," producing a glare from the spot lit piano.

The night owl hours limited the drinking fun to after hour parties and happy hours. The latter meaning that we might be drunk at the beginning of our shift and have a few drinks during the night, always in the back room, out of view of the customers. Another drawback of the new gig was that we weren't fed at the Inn. This resulted in a diet high in vodka and low in food. We slept late, ate in the middle of the day, and then off to happy hour or straight to work.

Towards the end of the summer the general manager from the Wigwam resort in Arizona visited and offered winter season jobs to several of the staff at the Inn and Sand Bar. I thought long and hard about the idea of migrating between two naturally beautiful places where people had to dig deep to find something to be unhappy about. My travels had been limited to within an hour radius of Providence with the exception of a spring break drive to Florida. Arizona would be something completely different. My doubts revolved around the work hours and the fact that I had just one final semester at Bryant. I settled on the unknown possibilities of post graduation life and resumed my search for part-time employment for the upcoming semester.

The convenience store was out of business, so I leveraged my bartending skills into a stock boy job at the local package store. I didn't like the night shifts as it threw my class and library schedule off, but a job was a job and it filled the gas tank. It was a high volume store selling beer, wine, and liquor in the space of a small grocery store. The owner's name blared from a red neon marquee reflecting into front windows papered with weekly price specials. I thought I might be of value with a good working knowledge of the product lines, but the manager, Louie, treated me like it was my first job ever. Louie was in his early fifties and reported to work each day in black Sansabelt slacks, steel-toed factory shoes, and short sleeve dress shirt, topped off with the same burgundy, dandruff dusted cardigan sweater he wore every day. Louie squinted through black rimmed safety glasses as he directed customers inquiring about a dry white wine to the gallon jug of what he pronounced, "Cha-bliss" instead of Chablis. Meanwhile I was relegated to stacking cases of beer in the stock room. An experienced stock boy could slide the leading edge of a hand dolly under a stack of ten or more cases of beer with just the right tip and kick of the hand truck. A slight miscalculation meant cutting a can and spraying the contents on the floor requiring a cleanup and re-stack.

If Louie witnessed this he would send me into the cooler to shiver for an hour while re-stocking the endless rows of cold singles and quarts. He would frequently have me circling the aisles with the floor mop, or if agitated, sweeping up outside in front of the store. I hated sweeping the broken glass and debris outside. I was 21 and about to be a college graduate but had to endure shouting matches with a bum in the alley, or the sneers of customers looking down at me as they went in for their weekly "groceries" of half gallon bottles of bourbon and vodka. I made an angry vow that this would never happen again in my lifetime. I was going to be financially successful; it was at the top of my list.

Back at Bryant I had settled into a concentration in computer information systems. I was easily bored with accounting and was attracted more to the variety in automating different operating processes involved in running businesses. To do the job properly you had to know how the business worked. I confirmed my interest with an internship at the fire department where I prototyped a database inquiry system for retrieving hazardous material information about each commercial building in town. At the time, the information was in paper files on forms required from each business. With my system the dispatcher could query the information in various ways and relay the basics to the fire truck in route. This all seems antiquated with today's fire trucks and their on-board technology, but I got a real sense of satisfaction out of learning about the fire department and designing something in return.

I finished up a Bryant that winter with honors and more sufficient interview skills, learned in the dining rooms and bars of Cape Cod. The combination resulted in two job offers. One was from a defense contractor in Connecticut that offered a higher starting salary and an automatic six-month raise that would bring it to $20,000. The second was for $16,800 and required completion of a three-month training program. If you completed the training you had to sign a three-year promissory note for $9,000; if you didn't pass the training, you were fired. Can you guess which one I chose? Before you do, let me say the training program was in Washington, D.C., and after completion you had no idea of where in the United States you could be assigned. Yes, the unknown possibilities trumped the better pay and certainty of reporting to the chainlinked fence, defense compound in Connecticut.

Back at home briefly before shipping out to D.C. after the holidays, I felt a relaxing of the usual tensions. I'm not sure if it was Ed and Alice looking forward to some peace in their retirement, or whether it was that I had some solid prospects, but I felt their good wishes, even if they didn't agree with my choice of employer. I returned the Dodge to its intended use as a second car for fishing trips and started looking for transportation of my own. I didn't have funds for much, but again Aunt Mae helped out and got me into my '78 Jeep Renegade. It was red with a tan Levi's interior. I loaded my two interview suits and a bag of casual clothes into the back hatch and headed south down Interstate 95.

I arrived at a four story white office building in Bethesda, Maryland, on the appointed Sunday evening, following the very explicit instructions on picking up apartment keys and identification for the 12-week training period. This was Ross Perot's Electronic Data Systems and there was only one way to do things, his way. Ross had been a star salesman for IBM and was a Naval Academy graduate before starting EDS in the early 1960s. EDS had a twenty-year run of success and were now being acquired by General Motors. The goal of this training was not only to teach job skills, but also to create a military style corporate culture, at least with those who survived. We heard varying accounts of class success rates from 50 percent to 85 percent of trainees moving onto assignments in the field. The rules were simple.

For men:

1. No facial hair
2. Haircuts off the collar
3. No tassels on your shoes
4. Dark suits, and ties

And a new twist, pastel shirts instead of white only.

For women it was much the same excluding hair restrictions, but with the addition of skirt length rules. You would be graded on assignments with a system of check-plus, check, or check-minus. If they didn't like anything about your performance you would be fired.

My classmates were from all over the eastern U.S. from a wide variety of academic backgrounds. Some had previous experience at EDS's accounts; others like myself were new to the company. The training regiment was an early start to a long day of classroom sessions, followed by assignments designed to keep you at the computer center downstairs until late in the evening. Everyone seemed on edge in this strict environment, afraid to do or say the wrong thing. On that first Monday of class we were required to stand up and introduce ourselves. In between the nervous quiet and the halting introductions, I noticed a guy in the front row who was wearing khakis and a brown sweater. I thought to myself, "This guy really has some balls, but I don't think he'll last long with these uptight corporate guys." When he was called on to introduce himself, he casually said it was obvious he'd forgotten his suitcase. He seemed to take it in stride. Right then I made a note to hang out with this guy, I liked his attitude.

I cruised through the first three of four weeks of training because most of the material was not new to me. Seven-day workweeks of extended hours were required by the full syllabus, but I was able to make a pact with Tim, of the brown sweater, and his roommate that we would take Sundays to see D.C. and have some fun. We were the only ones that added this item to the class schedule. On Sunday afternoons we would jump in my Jeep and drive around to see some sights, then find the local bars or go to Georgetown and let loose, before returning to the grind the next morning.

The training program was designed to keep you under pressure for an extended period and then bring that pressure to a climax at the deadline for three large complex programming assignments. These planned roadblocks would be the hurdles you were measured by in order to advance through the training. As the first deadline approached 90 percent of the class was struggling with the instructor, also new to the company, who we doubted could complete the assignment himself. My classmates started working overnight shifts and groggily shuffled into class each morning. I thought it was obvious they needed to fire the instructor and many classmates complained openly to the class manager, but we were mired in the bastion of an inflexible culture. I had learned a lesson long ago at the Seekonk Speedway, just because you're in charge, it doesn't mean you're smart. The vast majority of the class did not complete the assignment with accurate test results. The class manager spoke to the class the following week and admitted they hadn't provided the proper instruction on the assignment and we were not all going to be fired.

Our training classes occupied one floor of EDS's Government Systems building in Bethesda and when we left that floor for any reason we were all on our toes. The executive in charge of this division of EDS, "Mr. Chips," was one of two or three of Ross Perot's top lieutenants and headquartered on the fourth floor. He was a short and stocky man with dark features and brooding glare. His appearance was fastidious. Expensive, dark, perfectly tailored suits were always buttoned to reveal the minimum of a bright white shirt and red tie. The glint of monogrammed cufflinks bounced off the mirrored shine of polished shoes. He never had a hair out of place. Our class manager, administrative assistant, instructors, and any other employees we encountered from the other floors, feared contact with him and seemed to quiver or snap to attention in his presence. His meticulousness carried over into the office décor and hygiene. In the front lobby hung a giant painted eagle, our corporate symbol, looking over spotless floors and sparkling windows. You couldn't walk through the building without finding a seemingly permanent crew of painters whitewashing some hallway or office.

As we moved into the next phase of training with a new instructor, I volunteered to help bring up binders of new materials for the class. I put two boxes on a hand truck and wheeled them through the first floor lobby and into the elevator. On the ride up to the sixth floor classrooms, the elevator paused at the fourth floor, and Mr. Chips stepped in. He didn't say anything when I looked up, but tried to burn holes through my cheap navy blue suit with his eyes. I stared right back thinking, "What makes this little guy so tough?" I didn't realize how close I was to a premature end to my EDS career. He exited the elevator on the next stop and I continued on one more stop. I unloaded the boxes in the classroom and was ready to bring the hand truck back down when I heard shoes scurrying across industrial carpeting, threatening to spark a fire. Our class manager entered and with fear painted on her face said:

"Make sure you use the service elevator when you bring anything up or down!"

In the 60 seconds since I he had left the elevator, Mr. Chips had called up and given our manager an earful. Coming off the service elevator in my suit, I made it a point to lean back against the lobby wall, planting the sole of my shoe leaving a dark footprint. I would check it each day to see if Mr. Chips had sent the painters over yet.

As we neared the completion of our next segment of training the last big project was to send some students into all night working sessions again. I didn't stay up all night to cram during college, and I certainly wasn't about to do it here. Based on the class's lack of success on the previous big assignment, I thought there would be more firings by this point in the program. I was starting to think the 50 percent failure rate talk was just a scare tactic, since all my classmates were still here with only one exception. After this deadline we would be getting a "break weekend" before starting the final phase of training. We could turn in the assignment for instructor feedback beginning three days before the deadline, which I did. I knew I could make the corrections/improvements before the Friday 7 p.m. deadline, and made plans with Tim and his roommate to drive down to the Outer Banks in North Carolina for the weekend. We would drop off our assignments at noon and get a head start on the drive.

On Thursday morning our instructor made an announcement in class reminding us to have our assignments ready for her on Friday at 7 p.m. She repeated herself and then clarified that each of us would be required to hand the assignment to her in person at that time. And only at that time, and not a second earlier. She had gotten wind of our weekend plans and was throwing an unnecessary wrench into them, but why? Wasn't this about doing the assignment right, the "EDS" way, the way we were drilled on every day? Were we violating some military style cultural code by striving to complete something in order to enjoy the weekend? I suppressed the choice words running through my brain, that if spoken would lead to an instant firing. On Friday evening I was there handing in my assignment. It just happened to be the same copy the instructor had reviewed on Wednesday and included her red-penned comments without my corrections. I didn't get to North Carolina. You can't always get what you want. I got the instructor's point, now hopefully she was getting mine. I knew the assignment was close enough to pass.

On the following Monday I was called into the class manager's office. Sitting in my chair, I was surrounded by the class manager, my instructor, and another unknown manager. I wasn't as uncomfortable as they would have liked as my mind harkened back to detention hall. I let them do most of the talking:

"We don't let just anybody through this program."

"Why didn't you make the corrections the instructor asked for?"

"This lack of effort is unsatisfactory."

The instructor had gotten my point and it had obviously stung, but there was no need for me to confess my intentions. Push came to shove when I heard:

"I'm not sure we can let you continue in the program."

"You haven't proven a *complete knowledge* of the subject."

I finally said that I did have a complete knowledge of the subject, Assembler Language coding. They responded that the unfinished product did not prove this. I said they should look at the test results. Each of the three major subjects in the training program required a closed book written exam. It seemed they had not considered this idea previously as my instructor reached for her grade book. Blank looks replaced their practiced scowls as the instructor pointed to my name and the 97 percent mark next to it. It was the highest score in the class. The consternation in their eyes was now directed towards the instructor, feeling they had been brought in unprepared. I liked to think of it as not having a *"complete knowledge"* of the facts. I was quickly dismissed from the meeting with a warning.

They finally did get me to stay up all night. One of the last exercises was supporting an application running overnight at the data center. They would queue up various errors to crash the application and have you fix one problem after another all night. I did this successfully and quickly showered and headed for class. The class manager addressed us and told us we had a special guest this morning. None other than Mr. Chips would be speaking to the class that morning, to inspire us as we graduated and moved on to our job placements the next week. I struggled with his monotone delivery and diverted my eyes to the desktop in front of me. The faux wood grain of the laminate tabletop looked like waves hitting the beach. I rested my head on my hands.

When I opened my eyes, a sarcastic voice said, "Well, I see I only lost one of you today. Good luck."

And with that he was gone. The next week I opened the envelope with my new job assignment. It said "Detroit." It seemed they had gotten the last laugh.

# Motor City

I was now a college graduate with a job, a Jeep, and a set of new places, people, and experiences waiting. This feels like both the finish and starting line of my race to independence. From this point forward I commit to having fun on the journey. My mood is brightened. I made it! My quest to learn the lessons of a good life through observation and calculation is complete. I'm a smart guy with a world of opportunity in front of me. There is one problem though. It seems my list of lessons might have a few holes in it. If you view every encounter in life as a competition and every person a competitor, you'll always be in a struggle. You are also bound to lose more than you win, and what if you're not a good loser? I may need to adjust my approach. A couple of people might need to intervene and point out the difference between intelligence and wisdom. In the process maybe a little bit of the latter will seep in.

I steered the Jeep Renegade through western Maryland, Pennsylvania, and Ohio, approaching Detroit from the south. My knowledge of Detroit was sparse, and from the south side it looked very much like the "murder capital" of the United States. I stopped for gas on an exit off Interstate 75 called Wyoming, but was sure I wasn't *that* far west. The station attendant tried to sell me a Detroit Tiger's World Series commemorative baseball with my fill-up. They had won the 1984 Series the previous fall. I told him he had the wrong guy and pointed to my Rhode Island license plate. As I drove north the surroundings steadily improved until I found my assigned hotel in the suburb of Sterling Heights. I would spend a couple of months at this hotel because of the influx of technology workers to the automotive industry. With the large number of EDS people coming in to GM, there was a shortage of apartments.

I reported to the GM Technology Center campus the next day to find three of my classmates along with three others from an earlier class in Dallas. We had the final phase of our training to complete. Hands on programming work for nine to 12 months was required in order to graduate to full Systems Engineer status. We were the only non former-GM employees in this building newly adorned with an EDS logo and were all assigned the same office, an executive office with a secretary's desk out front in the open foyer. Four of us sat at desks in the interior office, while three others shared the open space out front. Our primary assignment was to find apartments and we were encouraged to use the workday to search and tour apartment complexes to discover any pending vacancies. It was not unusual to find us with newspapers sprawled open and feet up on the desks, sometimes looking at apartment listings, other times the sports and entertainment pages. We could go out touring unfamiliar suburbs and be lost for hours. My friend from class, Tim, was in the group and stationed the same hotel.

We were assigned into a group called "Internal Systems" which encompassed the software used to run the GM corporate data center, which occupied the first floor of our building. We had very little knowledge of this software, and almost no encounters with it or our manager during the first couple of months. While it was fun for a twenty-two year old to get paid to find an apartment, we all started to be concerned about not having any real work or a path to graduation. We eventually voiced this concern and were assigned to a new, first-time supervisor, who would construct a program for us to complete in order to graduate. Jimmy Walker shared a remarkable resemblance to his namesake on the *Good Times* television show with one exception: he was a five foot five inch white guy. He had the overbite, glasses, and goofy persona in common with black J.J., but he added pinstriped suits with the pants worn well above his waist to create "high waters." To hide his social awkwardness he went overboard with high-pitched, ebullient bursts of friendliness.

"Hello! You fellas having a good morning!" could be often heard with a mild slur due to his overbite. We didn't mind the friendliness at all, but we did mind the snail's pace of work assignments in this program of his. No matter how efficiently we completed simple tasks, we couldn't ramp up the frequency or difficulty of assignments. There were seven smart guys sharing the same office, and all bored to tears. This left plenty of downtime for each of us to perfect a dead on impersonation of our supervisor. Every day one of us would let loose with a monologue of his catch phrases, born out of frustration and boredom.

One remedy for the boredom was an old standby, happy hour. Our whole team would pile into the bar across the street on a Thursday or Friday afternoon. Barry from Seattle could grab a beer glass with his eyeteeth, crane his head back, and drain the contents hands free. Dave from California, and Cory from North Carolina could tell a good joke. The rest of us had Jimmy Walker impressions to fall back on. One afternoon, after many, many rounds, we fell into quoting movie lines. A very popular recent movie was *Stripes* with Bill Murray taking over the training for a bunch of misfit army recruits. I looked around the table and the similarities were too obvious to ignore. I launched into a familiar line from the movie trailer in a mock commanding voice.

"What kind of training are you boys doing?" In unison the guys responded, substituting "Walker" for "Army."

"Wal-ker Train-ing, sir!" They shouted back in military cadence.

I repeated the call, this time sliding my loosened tie up around my forehead like a bandana. The response was even louder. Then I started the song from the movie:

"There she was just-a walk-in down the street!"

Roaring back at me was the "Do-wa-diddy, diddy-dum, diddy-dee!" chorus. By the second line we were on our feet in a drunken march around the tables. Bartenders and staff jumped to their feet and shouted for us to leave. We marched straight out the doors into the parking lot, breaking into laughter. The ridiculousness of our display matched our circumstances. A comically dull work environment had replaced our intense training experience. Something had to change.

Spring turned to summer and slowly we were presented with other opportunities. Several guys split off to join the support team for GM's photographic division. Others worked on moving the commercial processing out of the data center down to an EDS corporate one in Texas, and then supporting the engineering systems that remained. In one of our team meetings, we were told of a temporary assignment available with the hardware-planning group for the data center. I didn't think any of these opportunities matched our intended career paths of application programming, but I really needed work to fill my days. I took the four-month assignment.

The hardware-planning group consisted of three guys responsible for managing changes to the hardware and software, and planning major upgrades to the computers, peripherals, and infrastructure of the data center. This was far removed from my training in applications programming, but I received a crash course in the workings of a data center. After each weekend's scheduled change window, we would update diagrams depicting the physical and logical connections of all the equipment, and distribute them to each department in the data center.

I was shown the ropes by the youngest member of the team, Rick, a co-worker about five years my senior. Each week we would walk the office space stopping in network security, tape operations, system software, or the IBM vendor offices to drop off updated copies of these printed reference diagrams. At every stop Rick had a friendly exchange with someone in each department. It could be about work, or the weather, or his beloved Detroit Tigers, but it was unanimous that Rick was well liked.

One week we were stopped in the hall by a vendor and told about an unplanned change they would be making that weekend. They hadn't done the preliminary steps to allow the change to be scheduled around other vendor and internal changes and were not assigned a given weekend timeslot. It was not an emergency and Rick told the guy the change wouldn't be going in on the weekend. The guy got hot and protested vehemently, but Rick was unbending and returned the animus with a stoic expression. The guy threatened escalation to management, even name dropping the name of the data center manager. Rick called his bluff offering to dial the phone. That was the end of the conversation and we moved on to the next stop.

It seemed my friendly mannered co-worker could be tough when needed, even adopt an attitude when pressed by a wrong-minded colleague. Maybe my Maditude could be reserved for a similar use. Could I bring it out only in reaction to strong-armed tactics or in situations where I was clearly in the right? I decided to try to emulate Rick's approach in the workplace, but I still needed to work on getting used to a positive default interaction with people. I was noticing this pleasant, polite, friendly manner occurring not just in the office, but also in interactions outside of work. You could be in a bar and go the men's room and the guy at the next urinal might start chatting about the football game or the weather. It was very different from my east coast experience, where I always felt two sentences away from a fight.

I grew to appreciate this aspect of midwestern life. I settled into an apartment across from a movie theater. They ran Sunday morning matinees starting around 10 a.m., so poorly attended that most weeks I had a private screening of a new release. I continued to absorb a working knowledge of how a data center operated while happily putting in a few extra hours keeping statistics, weekend change logs, or anything that might help Rick get to his evening graduate school studies on time. It reminded me of Mr. Capaldo's 9th grade biology class. I didn't mind being told what to do as long as I was learning and enjoyed the work.

That first spring in Michigan, the fourth member of our Bethesda training class, Cliff had an idea borrowed from his days growing up in South Carolina. Why not get a bunch of beer and spend the day floating down a local river. Cliff led the planning and Tim, Cory, and I quickly agreed. Cliff found a spot that rented canoes for a daytrip down the Au Sable River, which was a couple of hours' drive north. We pulled into the gravel parking lot on a Saturday in early April under a canopy of gray metal skies. The clouds were spitting at us and the temperature was not threatening fifty degrees. This was no South Carolina spring day. Undeterred, we loaded the cooler of beer into one canoe with Cliff and me. Tim and Cory took a second one along with plastic bags of cigarettes and cigars. Cory had his camera strapped around his shoulders. We confirmed the pickup place and time in the late afternoon with the driver, before his pick-up truck sped away.

The river was moving quickly this time of year due to the runoff of snowmelt. We were on the river less than ten minutes when Cliff needed to borrow a lighter from the other canoe for his cigar. Tim held onto an overhanging branch to halt progress as we approached from up stream. We weren't able to stop our momentum completely. As Cliff reached for their boat, the river had a bit too much propulsion and the miscalculation was proved disastrous. The two canoes collided and in an instant ours was overturned with Cliff completely submerged. I felt the icy water rush into my boots, and somehow, in mid-flip, I latched onto the crossbar of Tim and Cory's boat. Their canoe was now listing to nearly 90 degrees and they leaned back to try to counter my weight. Cigarettes were dropped and cameras clutched, as I struggled and splashed. With shock in their eyes they screamed:

"Get off!"

"Let go!"

They even attempted to knock me off with paddles. In one final panicked thrust, I slammed the canoe back level, propping myself across it and avoiding the icy plunge.

I settled in as a third passenger and our attention returned to Cliff. The overturned canoe had come to rest on a nearby bank. Cliff was downstream in knee high water fetching Budweiser's out of the river like a grizzly bear catching salmon. We put the cooler back together with the recovered beer and set off again downriver. In about thirty minutes I looked back at Cliff to see blue lips hiding chattering teeth, and made him take my precious sweatshirt. I was cold, but he looked like hypothermia was a possibility. We eventually decided to beach the canoes and found a spot to build a fire. The lighters were useless in lighting the now wet cigarettes, but came in handy for the fire. Once we got it going, Cliff warmed up by it in his birthday suit as we wrung out his clothes and laid them out by the fire. After an hour or so, we had him somewhat comfortable and returned to the boats to complete the trip. The next time Cliff suggested a canoe trip, and he did, we made sure it was in June.

Rick invited me to play in an occasional softball tournament or golf outing when there was an open spot. I had a built in social network of my classmates from EDS training with the common thread of all being new to the area. We had fun bar hoping, hosting parties, watching football games and I found many opportunities for dating. I would suffer good-natured kidding about my accent, and the jokes that ended with, "I didn't know they had a school in Rhode Island." It seemed I was the first person from Rhode Island that anyone had met.

"Hey, this guy's from Rhode Island."

"Yeah, say something, say something."

I was aware that I sounded different and could only joke back about them drinking "pop" instead of soda, but there was little else obvious in their Michigan twang. I was frequently reminded why most of the major television broadcasters had Midwestern roots. I started making an effort to better enunciate and insert "r"s into the appropriate places, sometimes resulting in comical tongue twisters.

At the end of the four months I was returned to Jimmy Walker and the internal systems team. I pushed for some graduation criteria as the holidays approached, but was unable to get anything finite. I wanted to get beyond the trainee status and look for some meaningful work involving how business systems could be automated to improve operation. Something like my experience at the fire department or even some system automation of the data center business processes. I had a flashback to my political science lecture. Jimmy Walker and his boss had "absolute power" and there wasn't anything I could do about.

January dragged into February and March with the snow piles turning gray and tired, but refusing to disappear. I was in limbo waiting for some blessing of graduation and not interested in the small mundane tasks that trickled my way. The group was smaller and most of the efforts involved migrating the data center workload to a Plano, Texas data center. In the middle of this work, I was given graduate status without any discernible reason and without any change in compensation. When the migration was finished in the late spring there was even less to do.

I kept in touch with Rick and started playing golf on Sundays with his group of eight or twelve guys. My game was rusty and sporadic. I was frustrated that I couldn't play at near the same level I had in high school. My Maditude would boil up into fits of swearing and club throws. As the season wore on my game declined further into a maelstrom of ill-tempered consternation. If you believe as I do that golf is a test of how you handle adversity, I was failing. It's a difficult game where even your best shots can take bad bounces, let alone your mistakes. My impatience at work was magnified on the golf course.

Rick was still in graduate school at night when he was promoted into his first leadership position, running the financial team for the data center. It was a challenging environment since the migration of the commercial workload left an oversized data center not able to recover its costs. Rick needed to add some technical skill to his team to implement a new billing application and develop the algorithms to charge for resource usage by the now engineering-only client accounts. He asked me if I was interested and I jumped at the chance to work in any application environment. I thought we had worked well together as teammates. We worked every day that October in preparation for the January 1 implementation. I didn't mind the hard work because I was again learning and interested in the topic. At the end of the year I received my first bonus from the data center manager and Rick. A new set of golf clubs!

For all intents and purposes I was doing well, was financially independent, and enjoying life. I bought myself a new GMC truck with my corporate discount, a TV and stereo for my apartment, and some better quality work clothes. All things I felt I deserved and had planned on while sweeping up in front of that liquor store. The problem was I didn't really earn much in comparison to my living expenses and I saw a long stretch of credit card payments ahead.

The new golf clubs meant more to me than a bonus, it was personal. Someone had thought about what would be impactful beyond the monetary value of the bonus; that was Rick. Rick was smart and hard working. He was a sports fan, especially baseball, which he had played at a high level. He followed the Tigers like I did the Red Sox. His favorite boyhood player was hall-of-fame right fielder Al Kaline. Mine was Red Sox hall-of-fame left fielder Carl Yastrzemski. Detroit is a great sports town, its hockey, football, and basketball teams are avidly followed, but there was something about a baseball town that made me feel at home. Michigan also had the most golf courses per capita in the United States and I started to explore more of them with annual outings in Northern Michigan. I worked for Rick for the next eighteen months and found I could bounce almost anything off of him. I felt comfortable seeking advice on my finances or how to handle a particular person or situation at work.

During this period of working together, his team evolved from a data center-based team to a field support team for a large group of human resources applications. I was still looking for a role in business applications work rather than on a support team. Rick not only agreed, but also gave me a strong recommendation and the freedom to interview with all the application teams. I thought this might be the chance to get to the job I had originally signed up and trained for. The problem was every team manager I spoke with wanted to know about my application's experience, which was limited to the data center billing system and using different technology than the human resources apps. I thought this was a very shortsighted bias. I thought the six months that remained on the promissory note, when I signed up for the training program, was also being used against me. My reaction was predictable. They weren't going to tell me what I could and couldn't do.

I consulted with Rick outside the office environment and in return I got advice that was tantamount to "You've got to do what is best for you." We both knew my options were better outside of company at this particular point in time. Rick would not be favorably judged, having a high performing team member leave the company, but this did not factor into his counsel. In my tortoise-paced evolution in people skills, I recognized something unique was in play. I could trust Rick. The list of people I felt I could trust had started and ended with Aunt Mae.

I quickly secured new employment with a large consulting firm that would bring me back to the East Coast. I bounced from Boston to New York on business applications projects that even included travel to Switzerland. I lived in New York City for a year and spent every free minute soaking in the culture and revisiting scenes from *Midnight Cowboy*, *Taxi Driver*, *Dog Day Afternoon*, and other favorite films set in the city. At work, I learned to decompose systems into their logical business rules and redesign them for new technologies. I excelled at this and had a voracious appetite for learning how every part of each business area worked. I didn't mind the highly aggressive, fast-talking East Coast managerial styles, because I enjoyed the work and the opportunity to learn.

I kept in touch with Rick and shared some of my excitement of my skill set expansion. He had been promoted to manage a larger group consisting of applications support teams. I told him about the interesting customer work I did in Switzerland and how the partners in the firm would fly over on the Concorde for review sessions. But when the highflying New York executives made a power play, making my home office in Boston a subsidiary of New York, things started to change. I was called into the New York office of my managing partner one day and told I was no longer considered on loan to the project from Boston. I would now be a regular employee of the New York office. I would no longer be on an expense account, but they were willing to give me a five thousand dollar raise. My expenses ran just over three thousand dollars, per month!

I was caught off guard and outmaneuvered while I was focused on the project work. I had little or no leverage since my Boston leaders now reported to these same New York partners. It seemed like this trust idea that I was introduced to with Rick, was as rare as I previously thought. I had that feeling again. The one when you feel you're getting pushed around and your instinct is to push back harder even if it hurts your own interests. I was in the middle of my one-month transition off expenses when I came to the idea to call Rick. Maybe I could apply some of these redesign techniques to applications he or one of his peers managed. I didn't want to leave the project work I was deeply involved with, but I didn't want to be pushed around either. Rick was agreeable and set up interview sessions with several managers in his division.

I was able to rejoin the EDS team working in the business applications area where I belonged and at a rate that was just shy of my New York offer. My New York partners were furious since we were in the middle of an important phase of deliverables. Yet I had a clear conscience because they had dictated the timing and forced a decision.

A few years later the phone rang in my Michigan office. It was a lawyer from a firm in New York, doing discovery for a lawsuit by his corporate client against my old consulting firm. There were accusations of overcharging of hours and expenses in the billing of the project I had worked on. Maybe the Concorde flights, cabaret visits, and daily parking fees in New York City were catching up with my former friends? Maybe I had used my Maditude at just the right time.

I settled back into life in Michigan with a bit more financial margin and took Rick's advice and joined the 401K, retirement savings plan. I felt I was traveling a long road to financial freedom, and this was a major stop along the way. I enjoyed happy hours, parties, and an active dating scene. There were softball teams from work and regular Sunday morning golf games. Even with all these social opportunities, I found great enjoyment in intermixing periods of solitude. I was completely content to stay home on a Saturday night and read, watch a film, or listen to music. As part of my cultural immersion in New York, I had gone to see Dizzy Gillespie and his trio at the famous Blue Note Jazz club in Greenwich Village. In Detroit, radio host Ed Love provided a broader education in jazz through his programs each evening on WDET public radio. I was reading books about the history and evolution of jazz and then started to collect CDs. I was particularly fascinated with Thelonious Monk, the notoriously difficult but brilliant jazz pianist. It seemed to me that jazz musicians ignored the structure and rules of their predecessors in music and followed their instincts, eventually gaining broad acceptance. This idea fed right into my feelings toward the power structures in society, whether it was at work, or church, or in politics. I was not a fan of the status quo.

During my geography and job changes, my group of friends from the EDS training program remained in Detroit and settled down. Tim's girlfriend Ellen from back home in Syracuse moved to Michigan and they were married before I left for Boston and New York. I met Ellen's sister Leslie on one of her visits to Michigan and again at their wedding in upstate New York. We dated for a while afterwards and she visited Michigan again.

Leslie and I were attracted to each other, but were complete opposites. She had a social work and public policy concentration in both her education and employment. She finished grad school in Pittsburgh and had stayed, finding work as a policy director for a non-profit. My focus was on economic policy, mainly my own. She was taken aback to see my closet full of dark suits, white shirts, and red ties, meticulously arranged. I was pro-business, tough on crime or any other behavioral variance that affected others. I believed we were all responsible for ourselves. She worked with female offenders. Her employer was a non-profit that tried to provide life skills and job training for offenders transitioning back into society. They also had lock-up facility that functioned as an incarceration alternative and a halfway house. Many of the women despised the very people and organization trying to help them. The recidivism rates for these women were astronomical.

We argued about my hard line approach of three strikes and you're out. I couldn't fathom how you could achieve any sense of job satisfaction in her work environment. We had almost nothing in common, but we did manage to laugh about our stark differences. Leslie volunteered one Friday night a month, answering calls on a crisis hotline.

"So, you get paid for this?' I asked.

"No, that's why it's called volunteering, stupid."

"Is it some sort of resume-building thing?"

"No, it's just something you do for the community."

"And you give up Friday night and stay up until 2 a.m.?" I countered.

"What don't you understand, should I talk slower?"

A few minutes later I would return to the subject in mock confusion.

"So you don't get paid for this?"

We would laugh, but both strongly hold on to our perspectives. Later in the evenings I would throw in another jab.

"So what's this community thing you speak of?"

She was easy company and there was something natural about being around her, but I was pretty protective of my long sought independence. We had the distance between Detroit and Pittsburgh to overcome if we were to keep dating and I was not completely open to the idea of having the steady influence of someone else in my life. I kept our time in the social fun compartment of life, without consideration for anything more. After some poor follow-up on my part, she moved on and began seeing someone steady in Pittsburgh. I focused on work and started pursuit of a graduate degree at night. The next several years are what are now known as "the time I needed to mature."

# Changing Course

Things are pretty good as this stage. I'm enjoying life as an information technology professional, a golfer, a baseball fan and I find just enough time to mix in some movies, books, and music. I feel no impulse to change a thing. I'm settled enough to have time to reflect on things. Not in any deep philosophical way, but more like a boxer on the stool in between rounds. Until now I was too busy fighting the fight to pause and assess.

It was a stormy Sunday morning with enough rain to cancel my usual golf game and the forty-five minute commute up to the course. I was busy with work and schoolwork the other six days of the week, but Sunday was always a day of relaxation for me. Even back at the Bataan training program in D.C., I managed to take most Sundays for myself. With the rain came more unanticipated time for myself. On the sofa in my rented house I pushed aside the books on critical decision-making and probabilities and grabbed a book of Robert Frost poetry. I had discovered him during countless afternoons in the campus library at Bryant. Looking for a break from textbooks, I would explore the library shelves and read about architecture, art, film, music, or literature for an hour before returning to studies. It seemed Robert Frost could describe what I felt when appreciating nature, through poems like "The Onset" or "Stopping by the Woods on a Snowy Evening." The paperback's creased binding made it open to another favorite of mine, "The Road Not Taken."

After contemplating Robert Frost's traveler craning to see down each path, and taking the grassy one less traveled, I dozed off. When I woke up the rain had stopped, leaving clouds and a light mist. I was hungry and decided to get some breakfast. I walked a block over to the main road into the parking lot of the Pancake House. I bought a Sunday paper from the box and joined the line of twenty or so along the front entrance.

I was absorbed with reading Red Sox box scores from the early spring season, when I was tapped on the shoulder. It was Tim's wife, Ellen saying hi. Tim, Leslie, and a friend from college, Brenda, soon joined her. They asked me to join them for breakfast, and I did. Afterwards they said they were heading for the zoo and I should come along. It had been years since Leslie and I dated and the atmosphere over breakfast seemed light and carefree, so I agree to go along and spend my newfound Sunday free time.

We walked the zoo grounds with Brenda providing comic relief. She did impersonations of several animals with both sound and facial expressions. When we got to the monkey exhibit I took center stage with a classic under bite monkey face. I also had the advantage of the same proportions as these creatures and got big laughs.

I had recently been upgrading my business attire, trying on new suits and being fit for alterations, when I encountered my least favorite tailor. He was a miniature Italian man with a pincushion in one hand and tape measure in the other. He motioned me up onto a round pedestal speaking only broken English. He pinned my cuffs and then ran the tape measure down my arm:

"Built like moonkey," he said.

I frowned but it was true, my 37" shirtsleeves left my hands hanging above my knees on my outsized 6'1" frame. I guess he was learning English by visiting the zoo.

We were leaving the primate area in the zoo when I read aloud a plaque describing how the female's butt would swell and turn pink during the mating period.

I said, "The same thing happens with humans, only the girl's butt swells *after* they mate."

This drew more laughs and only mock offense. They sure seemed easy to be around. At the end of the day Leslie asked me if I could join them that night at a club they were going to. I said sure without really thinking about it. We were both dating other people at the time, but were drawn to each other. It was an unintentional meeting, but from it, a very natural launch into dating each other again.

We still had the Detroit to Pittsburgh distance to overcome, but we made the effort and alternated the five and a half hour drives when we visited each other. As we spent more time together, I realized some of the differences in our approach to the world could be construed as two ways to get to the same place. If we both faced a theoretical conflict that had one of two monetary outcomes:

One:  You win $0; your opponent wins $100.

Or

Two: You lose $200; your opponent loses $100.

Leslie would always choose number one and feel good, emphasizing the conflict hadn't ended up costing her anything. I, on the other hand, would always choose number two, being certain to leave my opponent with the idea that the conflict had cost them something, regardless of my own costs. If Leslie had found that ten-dollar bill in the grocery store in 1972, she would have donated it to the Thanksgiving food drive, felt great about it, and not been mad at anyone.

Leslie approached almost all situations with an unbridled zest to do what she felt was right, even if it opened her up to repercussions from opponents. Whatever damage they might inflict, she would deal with, and leave the opponent to live with their actions. I, on the other hand, would never consciously give an opponent an opening to inflict damage, unless it was calculated to allow an even greater reprisal. I framed everything into a win-lose scenario and took the losses hard. Leslie thought of everything in an "I win or they lose" scenario. This approach came with a freedom of conscience, but also required a different kind of toughness. It asked the question: are you tough enough to expose yourself to the negative outcomes others may create? She had to accept that they could walk away feeling they had won, even if she felt they lost because of their negative behavior.

I was no easy convert to her way of thinking, but as we grew closer, I developed a sincere respect for her approach. You had to have some trust in human nature. You can give everyone a chance to react well, and you can try to understand his or her point of view. Rick had taught me that this trust thing, so foreign to me, could be a very important part of life. Leslie and I could always laugh about our differences, but our mismatched personality traits were somehow blending into a bigger whole.

The frequency of our Detroit-Pittsburgh commutes increased and it became harder to separate at the end of weekends. After asking about my weekend and hearing a recount of another trip to Pittsburgh, a female friend at work said, "Oh, you're in love."

I think I scowled, but she was right. We weren't supposed to be using words like that. I had some troubling thoughts I needed to reconcile. I went back to my legal pad and made a list:

Positives:

1. I want to spend all my free time with Leslie

2. I want to stop driving to Pittsburgh

3. I have a house here that we can both live in

4. I trust Leslie implicitly

Negatives:

1. I would be letting someone have unprecedented influence on my life

2. I worked too hard for this freedom to give it up

3. I vowed never to bring anyone else's life down with anger or anxiety

These thoughts rattled around in my head. Maybe I wouldn't trouble her with fits of Maditude, these incidents were becoming rare. I was stretching to see down each life path as far as I could, and choose the one less traveled, and yes, it would make all the difference. I, the master of reading human instinct, was ready to make an important phone call to Leslie, and ask her that special question, "What do you think about moving to Detroit?"

I was basking in the radiance of my brilliant deductive skills, when the answer came through the handset speaker:

"Why? I mean…I have a house here, my job?"

I countered with living in my house, but that led to a discussion of working in social services in Detroit. That would be a tough job, for even Leslie. She didn't seem to see the brilliance in my thinking. Why wouldn't you give up your career and home, just for a chance to hang out with me? We talked around the idea for hours that night and each time it came back to "Why?" She was doing her best to tell me that she needed something more in her future, to give up what she had built in Pittsburgh. The time grew late and I was tiring when I took her final hint and said:

"So, you want to do the 'M' word?"

I didn't even have it in my vocabulary, but she rightly countered with:

"M as in move?"

I clarified in what should go down as the world's worst marriage proposal. Two a.m., on the phone, stuttering to say the word, and in shock, not due to the "Yes" answer, but that I had decided to go there. The next morning I called back.

"What happened last night?"

We laughed, but it was done. A more insightful person would have gotten there a lot sooner.

We made plans during the year for her to move in the next summer, before getting married that fall. I made a call to Alice and Ed and made plans for a short visit to allow them to meet Leslie.

When I made short visits home during holidays, Ed and Alice were a bit more at ease. I could feel their genuine rooting interest in me. They hoped I did well. At the end of visits, I even adopted a habit of shaking hands with Ed and giving Alice a hug. It's like we stopped being on opposing teams. With Leslie in the mix, we were able to focus solely on the present and future, and avoid discussion of many of the rough spots from the past.

Our visits always included a delicious Sunday dinner prepared by Ed, usually a roast with all the fixings. I had told Leslie about Ed's excellent cooking and she really appreciated it. This led to Ed's standard line, sitting at the table after dinner:

"Your girlfriend has quite an appetite!"

Leslie took it as the compliment it was meant to be. She even got used to Ed's conversational style of not using her name, and speaking of her in the third person, while sitting right next to her. They both took to Leslie's easy social style and grew very comfortable being around her. Once, with the three of them on a car ride, they erupted into a screaming match that startled Leslie. She saw a flash of their tempers at high volume, but it was an isolated incident. Most of our time together was pleasant. Leslie even went to church with Alice, although she had no religious affiliation and was brought up without any participation. Her favorite part of Catholic Mass was the exchange of "Peace be with you" with the surrounding parishioners towards the end of the service.

Back in Michigan I was beyond busy trying to manage a major application re-design and finish graduate school at night. I remember standing in the break room in the office, staring through the streaks of rain at blurred streetlights and the black asphalt parking lot, thinking, "I need some sleep." On the nights I wasn't in class, I was in the office until 9 or 10 p.m., and maybe back in during the night for production problems. I didn't mind the hard work for stretches, but I wished for that summer break on Cape Cod I used to look forward to. In my non-existent spare time I needed to get ready for Leslie's arrival and work on a plan for transferring within the company to a city where both Leslie and I could work. I had no luck getting a transfer to Pittsburgh and she still did not want to work in Detroit.

We were married in the fall and settled into an apartment and new jobs at the end of the year, in Boston. It was Leslie's choice of location and I could hardly disagree with being on familiar ground. I went to work in the cellular communications division and looked forward to learning about another new industry. After a year we moved into a newly built home in Foxboro, Massachusetts.

Rick had moved onto a new leadership role and was traveling around the U.S. I invited him to Boston for a weekend visit, timing it for a weekend when the Detroit Tigers were playing the Red Sox. The Red Sox had a good team coming off consecutive playoff appearances in the early 1990s. I tried any and all ticket avenues for decent seats at Fenway, from old college friends, from people in the office, but no luck. I could buy tickets at the box office, but only bleacher seats, which I did. I was sure I could make a deal with the scalpers on the streets surrounding the ballpark.

On the Saturday of the game we took the early train into Boston. It was a time when they were cracking down on scalping and there were endless cops circling the ballpark. I left

Rick and Leslie across the street and started to covertly inquire with scalpers. I walked the street with one for a stretch while bargaining, then back in the opposite direction with another, trying to make a deal. Finally I was able to trade the bleacher seats and 50 bucks for box seats on the third base side. The scalper had me follow him along Lansdowne Street and duck into a notch in the back of the Green Monster wall to make the exchange out of sight. I returned, all smiles, to Rick and Leslie across the street. I hoped Rick would experience that same flash of bright green charm I did on my first Fenway visit. They were all giggles from witnessing my display of illegal commerce.

The seats were good and not too far from the visiting Tiger's dugout. After the game we walked over to the Sheraton lobby lounge and had drinks. While we were sitting there a man crossed the lobby on his way into the sports bar on the main level. He wore slacks, loafers, and a dress shirt with a mandarin collar. The collar was a short standing band of less than an inch and open in the front. This shirt style was beginning to make a comeback in the fashion cycle. I looked above the collar to recognize Al Kaline, the retired Tiger great, now doing television commentary for the Detroit station.

"Hey, Rick, there's Al Kaline," nodding in that direction.

Rick glanced up: "That's not Al Kaline."

"Sure it is, I recognize him from the Tiger broadcasts."

"That's not Al Kaline."

"Really, you want to bet."

"How 'bout the drink tab."

"Sure, how you gonna prove it."

"How do you know it's not him, visiting teams stay at the Sheraton all the time."

"Al wouldn't wear a shirt like that."

"OK, follow me I'll introduce you."

I understand the feeling you might get if you run into a boyhood hero and it's a bit jarring to realize how old they are now, and how old it makes you feel. What I didn't get was how you knew what he would wear. Al had disappeared into the Sheraton bar by the time I coaxed Rick into following me in there. I was confident and looking forward to meeting Al Kaline, but didn't want to disturb his conversation with several guys at the bar. Rick waived off the whole introduction idea when we realized Al was talking with Tiger All-Stars Alan Trammel and Mike Henneman. Several other teammates were also at the bar and Rick didn't want to intrude. Back at the table, Rick, with drink tab in hand, had to admit the guy with the shirt was Al Kaline.

A couple of years later, I was traveling on business to Detroit and in the same building as Rick's office. I decide to swing by on the odd chance he wasn't on the road himself. I walked through a maze of cubicles and found a center row of manager offices. I followed the office layout scheme to locate the number the front desk guard had given me. As I passed one office, a narrow pane of glass next to a closed door revealed Rick's familiar silhouette. Rick's back was to the door and he was busy typing on his computer. I was about to knock when I noticed something, Rick's shirt. It had a mandarin collar! I knocked twice and stuck my head into his office. "Al Kaline wouldn't wear a shirt like that."

After a few years working in the cellular communications division, I realized this acquired piece of the EDS Corporation operated in a different culture. There was little flexibility and room for advancement. Soon after moving to Boston, Rick had asked if I was interested in joining a team he was assembling to start-up a new client engagement. I helped with some deliverable reviews, but was reluctant to commit to the extensive travel required, especially being newly married. But now I felt it was time to try something new and I inquired with Rick on their progress and if there was any possible role for me.

It wasn't long before Rick had a position in mind for me. I was managing a small team in Boston, but Rick gave me responsibility for a larger team, budget, and customer deliverables. It was a chance to learn another set of business processes, this time in logistics and warehousing. For the next six years I traveled full time, working long hours, but enjoying the work and learning all the time. We built, tested, and successfully implemented new business applications and processes all over the country. With that success came rewards in many forms. Yes, there were monetary rewards in salary, bonus, and advancement, but also intangible rewards. We were able to construct a team that operated with Rick's model that business was personal. You needed to know your team, customers, and peers and supervisors personally. You needed to understand what was most important to them and find ways to create win-win outcomes for the business, customers, and employees. Rick was held out as an example across the company in how to achieve this balance amongst these often competing agendas. On every step of the journey, Rick avoided the limelight and re-directed the corporate praise to his team members, giving us even greater opportunities for advancement.

We found out that Rick really wasn't seeking corporate fame. I'm certain he did very well financially, but it would be hard to detect, riding in his pick-up, from his one bedroom apartment, to the public golf course he was playing. He wasn't interested in the trappings of success and it taught me a valuable lesson. If you are comfortable and confident in who you are, there is no need to advertise your success in how you live. I didn't try to follow Rick's model; I tried to understand what was important and natural to Leslie and me, and live my life that way.

In our case it meant living below our means and building a long-term financial base. It was a lesson in ignoring my natural competitive tendencies. It also helped that I was getting exposure to many experienced high-level leaders in EDS. It seemed the more successful they were in the corporation, the more likely they were to be on their third wife, or second heart attack. I knew that my definition of success was based on freedom, happiness, and financial independence.

Leslie added to this equation, including community citizenship and giving back. In her view we had all we needed.

With all the travel and long hours I would occasionally get the longing for an extended break, like my summers on Cape Cod. With our extra financial resources in mind, I convinced Leslie to look at cottages on the Cape. The volatile real estate cycle of the northeast was closer to bust than boom, and I thought with my knowledge of the area I could find a bargain. We soon realized we were out of our league in looking at coastal properties. We could only afford a cottage that would be washed into the Atlantic in a decade, or one that was literally falling down and required complex permitting and major renovation. I excluded condos or landlocked inland properties. I wanted something to remind me of the natural beauty of the area, preferably near the National Seashore.

We were close to defeat when we extended our search and viewed a cottage three lots back from a small public beach access to Cape Cod Bay. It was more than $100,000 above our budget but had a recent price drop and was on the outer Cape convenient to the Atlantic side of the National Seashore. It was in working order but required a new deck, immediately. It also came with a long history of summer rentals, many recurring. I used all my power of persuasion to convince Leslie we could afford the place if we kept it rented all summer. We put in an offer and reached an agreement with the elderly couple selling it. They had not seen it in more than a decade.

I was busy working and traveling. Leslie was working and commuting in Boston every day. Our weekend rendezvous were something out of *Planes, Trains, and Automobiles*. I left Leslie with the responsibility to work with the rental agent on keeping the place occupied and using the summer income to pay the mortgage and utilities. I kept claiming the place would soon be cash flow neutral, but it never seemed to happen. Even as the economy improved and rents increased, we seemed to have renovation and repair bills that had to come out of our pockets. When we did spend time there, in the border seasons of June and September, I would aggravate Leslie with noisy renovations that made it feel anything but a vacation. I tried to convince Leslie we were building substantial equity in the place using the evidence of our rising property taxes.

With our property investment and the additional income from my success at work, we were able to do a couple of other small things. We would put Ed and Alice on the rental calendar each June, still in the border season, but in the long daylight days when Ed traditionally took vacation. They could avoid the crowds of summer and feel like they had a summer cottage themselves.

I was usually so worn out with work and traveling, the only place I wanted to be was in my own bed. Leslie would occasionally meet me where I was working and to give me a break from flying. Sometimes it was a condo with views of Alcatraz, other times it was Akron. For her the novelty of a weekend getaways wore off quickly. We decided to take a week's vacation and hatched a plan to meet in San Francisco and drive down to Monterey. With all my frequent flyer miles stacking up we talked about adding a wrinkle to the plan. What if we had Leslie, who was flying from Boston, take Ed with her? We could deliver him to his sister's place in Santa Rosa for a visit. Ed was now in his late seventies, but still quite spry. He was always interested in traveling, and an escort from Leslie should ease any apprehensions. We were correct in our assumption that Alice would have no interest in the trip.

I met Leslie and Ed at the San Francisco airport after taking the much shorter hop from Las Vegas, where I was working. They were all smiles after a smooth flight in first class. As I navigated the rental car through the city, Ed kept remarking on how it looked different than he remembered from the last time he was there. It had been over 50 years since he was discharged in San Francisco after his service in World War II. We made it up to Santa Rosa and spent the day getting reacquainted with my aunt, uncle, and grown cousins, before leaving Ed to tour the wineries and sites of the Russian River landscape with them.

On the drive down to Monterey with Leslie, I enjoyed the account of the first class travel with Ed. She said he would remark on the small things we took for granted like the snacks, "You know these nuts are warm!"

She said when the flight attendant asked if he would like a glass of wine, and never a wine drinker, he said, "No, thanks."

Leslie leaned closer and whispered, "You know it's free."

"I guess I will have a glass."

Later when the flight attendant asked if he'd like another glass, it was, "Sure."

Our plan was having the effect I had hoped. This was something that was easy enough for us to do, but it created something out of the ordinary for Ed. I think I was getting a bigger kick out of it than anybody. It was a benefit from my work, in more ways than one.

Learning to manage other people well required you to put yourself in their shoes. In Rick's thinking, you needed to get to know them personally, understand their background, family, and approach to life. Understand their goals and dreams. When you had success, you needed to share it. But if you were really good, you might be able to reward people in more meaningful ways. What we didn't talk about, but what I learned through experience, was the tremendous satisfaction you get in the rare times in your career when you're able to pull this off. That ended up being a life lesson I could apply to all areas of life, outside of work. It gave me some insight into how Leslie must feel in organizing her endless community service projects. I was stealing this for my own use, and I got more satisfaction from it than Ed probably got from his visit to California.

I stayed extremely busy during this period. My weeks started with Leslie dropping me off to meet the 4:30 a.m. express bus to Logan Airport. On Fridays, I would take the subway into the city and meet Leslie near her office. We would walk or take a cab to another subway that took us to the train station. From there we rode the commuter train down to our local station where we retrieved our car from its rented space. After a fifteen-minute ride we were pulling into the driveway. The idea of commuting into Boston on weekends to take advantage of its myriad of entertainment opportunities was beyond our comprehension. I still yearned for that summer break and change of pace, but our seasonal Cape cottage needed to stay rented. The annual property taxes were now ten thousand dollars.

At work, there was another in the endless stream of re-organizations. This time the business unit-driven realignment created an opportunity for me to orchestrate a corporate sponsored move. Leslie's public policy work required residence near a state capitol, so we looked at and visited Austin, Texas, and Raleigh, North Carolina. We decided on Raleigh with its closer proximity to the northeast and better justification for working in my new business unit. We continued to be landlords for the Cape cottage and visited before and after the summer season for the next few years, doing handyman projects and winterizing it. At the end of the next season we finally relented and put the cottage up for sale. We realized we would never be able to summer on the Cape.

We interviewed several realtors and were surprised with the variety of assessments. The economy had been on an extended upturn along with real estate prices in the Northeast. Our listing agent thought we shouldn't do anything more to improve the place. It should sell as a seasonal cottage, needing updates. Later that winter she called with the good news of an offer. More than twice what we had paid for the place! Our timing was right and even after settling up with Uncle Sam, we would have a nice profit.

# Nothing to be Mad About

I finally got smarter and gained some wisdom through time and experience. It helped me reflect on my past and decide that it was worth sharing. I'm soon to discover that all the control and calculation in life planning is really a mirage. My path was both unique and common. All of our experiences with people, places, music, food, and culture are different, but we all share a common struggle to match the reality of our life with our pre-imagined picture of it. I think the most important thing a young person needs is a broad exposure to feed their imagination of the future. Add in the influence of people to help them learn about life along the way and you have my recipe for success. We can all be these people.

In 2004 my Boston Red Sox made history. They were the first team to overcome a 3-0 game deficit in the American League Championship series, and beat the evil empire of the New York Yankees, four games to three. They went on to sweep the World Series against St. Louis, four games to none, to become World Champions. Three years later they did it again sweeping the Colorado Rookies to win the World Series. On both occasions, a graying Carl Yastrzemski threw out the ceremonial first pitch of game one at Fenway Park. It had been 86 years of futility for the Red Sox, mostly attributed to the "Curse of the Bambino," the sale of Babe Ruth to the Yankees. They had been close a few times, losing the World Series in seven games in 1967, when I discovered them in kindergarten. They lost the exciting 1975 series to the Reds in seven games, as I was finding my way into my first year at junior high school. I was working my first job in Detroit in 1986, when that famous ground ball went through Bill Buckner's legs leading to a game seven loss to the Mets. These highlights were sandwiched between stretches of mediocrity, leading to my Uncle Jesse calling them "a bunch of hams."

Now they were two-time world champions and Uncle Jesse wasn't here to witness it. Cancer had taken him years earlier. He had retired from his custodian job at Oldham School and settled into a daily regimen of 7 a.m. mass, often walking to St. Francis each morning. I struggled to understand how he seemed so content with life, while I had been so unsatisfied and anxious to leave the same place. The answer would hopefully come with many years of life experience and some force-fed wisdom.

Leslie and I sat in the bar of a Greek restaurant on the East Side of Providence. We had just come from Ed's wake where she was introduced to my old childhood friend Stephen. Stephen walked us to our car that night and we exchanged information and pledged to try to get together sometime. I thought about my father and whether there was more to know about him than I discovered during his lifetime. As I got older, we would spend more time chatting about his younger days and his service in the navy during WWII. My early years were too full of anger and consternation for me to retain any clues on what Ed thought about his life as a father, not that they would have been shared.

Ed stayed in good health for all of his eighty-seven years and then left us in an instant. He was admitted into the hospital on a Friday evening suffering from a bad cold, and by

Sunday night he was gone. Alice had called that Sunday afternoon to tell me he was in the hospital and not doing well. Leslie and I raced home and booked the next flight to Providence, 6 a.m. the following morning. I was awoken at midnight with a call from the attending doctor at the hospital. He said they could keep Ed on life support until I arrived in the morning, but he would not recover. He said Alice was leaving it up to me to make the decision and he needed to know.

Ed hated hospitals and doctor visits and I knew the right decision was to not have him spend a minute longer in the hospital than he had to. After a shaky day of little sleep and bumpy travel to Providence, I was able to find solace in my decision. It was a blessing that he went quickly when it was his time, and didn't endure a long hospitalization. He would have been an awful patient.

I have the same dislike for hospitals as Ed. I'm not sure whether it's the idea of all the seriously ill people being collected in the same place, or the proclivity of unhappy endings, but I'm never comfortable. This feeling extends from the lobby and waiting rooms through the various departments in the place. I stay on edge, head on a swivel, looking to fend off the grim reaper about to spring out from around every corner.

When Leslie and I were still dating, she had an unwelcome development that required major surgery. It was a difficult procedure and a long recovery. Years later, soon after we had moved to Raleigh, the problem reoccurred. We faced the unpleasant choice of repeating the previous surgery or a more direct approach that would eliminate future problems, but it meant an end to child bearing. The latter offered a better quality of life without the body chemistry-altering medications. Leslie, always concerned more about others, asked about my feelings on ending our ability to reproduce. I never doubted that Leslie would be a great mother, but I still hadn't convinced myself that I should be an influence on any young person's life. I assured her I would be fine with the consequences, especially the results of a healthy, happy Leslie.

I put on my best impersonation of calm, supporting husband as I accompanied Leslie through the intake and pre-op process in the early dawn hours. I paced and fidgeted for a couple of hours in the waiting area, then rejoined her in a recovery room and finally in her own room. It was a straightforward procedure and went according to plan. I spent the rest of the day and the overnight in a chair in her room as she dosed in and out of morphine-induced sleep. After midnight the nursing staff changed over and I noticed a change in attitude. They would burst noisily into the room, flipping on the lights and raising Leslie's bed to take her temperature, or give her medicine. They were curt with her, and even less pleasant with me. I knew we were dependent on these people, but I added this to my list of why I didn't like hospitals.

In the early morning hours, Leslie convinced me to drive the 15 minutes back to the house to shower and change. She was back to sleep before I left the room. When I returned, refreshed and ready for our last day in the hospital, I found Leslie upright in bed, crying. She was in pain and a breakfast tray lay on the swing table, just out of reach. She had been trying to get to it, but the pain was too much. She had pressed the call button several times but no one had responded. I kicked myself for taking that ride for a shower. I calmed her and helped her with breakfast. After she settled back to resting, I set out down the hospital corridors.

I found a nurse's station, but no sign of any staff. I pounded my fist on the top of the counter, jarring clipboards, monitors, and everything else into a loud clamor.

"Hey!!!" I screamed.

Now I suddenly found a couple of staff members running my way.

"Sir, sir!"

"What the fuck is going on here!!!" I yelled. One of them happened to be the supervisor, which was obvious because she immediately threatened to call security. I glared at her. Look at me, keep looking at me, yes, you could call security but they aren't going to get here in time. Through gritted teeth I told her about my displeasure with the care we were getting and how that was going to change, "Right fucking now." I gave her our room number and let her know I would be there all day. My flash of anger was a relatively rare occurrence and reserved for circumstances where I felt bullied. It reached the boiling point when I sensed the other party felt I had no power and I wouldn't dare speak up. That's just the recipe for me to speak up and get aggressive. Other than these occasions, I think I'm just a sweetheart of a guy to be around. We had pleasant service for the remainder of the day and were luckily discharged before the evening shift change brought back any familiar faces from the previous night. Ed hadn't spent more than a few days in the hospital during his entire life, and I was glad for that.

Back in Raleigh after a week in Providence surrounding Ed's wake and funeral, we tried to settle back into normal routines. During a follow-up visit with Leslie's doctor, we received a shocking kick to the gut. We sat stunned and silent in his office as he explained the results of a biopsy that revealed a particularly nasty variety of cancer cells in her breast tissue. Surgery was the next step, but we were encouraged to get a second opinion. The diagnosis scared the hell out of both of us. We asked for and received a referral to a specialist at the major university hospital system nearby. The earliest appointment we could get was five weeks away. We couldn't fathom how you could receive news like that and wait five weeks to do something about it. We sat in the car pondering the future and trying to come up with another option. Our brains were numb as we tried to recall the details of what the doctor had told us. At a loss, I blurted out, "We could call Kristi." You may ask, who is Kristi? She and her husband Bob became very close friends after our move to Raleigh. She is a transplanted New Englander like myself and we have shared many stories about growing up that resonate with us both.

Leslie replied, "I was thinking the same thing."

"It's a lot to ask," I said tempering the enthusiasm for the idea.

"Yeah, but she would be great and with all her experience counseling cancer patients."

We dialed Kristi from the parking lot and Leslie's shaky voice repeated what we were told by her doctor. Kristi told us to come over right away and we went straight from the doctor's office.

Kristi had moved on from counselor to a representative for a pharmaceutical company's chemotherapy drugs. She told us what she would do if she were in our shoes. She would use the superb specialists and facilities that were right in the neighborhood. We told her about our referral into the same system and the five-week wait for an appointment. Kristi took over to become our general manager and started drafting a fantasy team of doctors to care for Leslie. It was dinnertime on a Thursday evening, but she reached for her phone and dialed the mobile number of one of the world's leading oncologists, specializing in this type of cancer. She asked for and received personal favors and turned our five-week wait into two days. We would be meeting with the oncologist on Monday. This was followed by calls to line up a consultation with a leading cancer surgeon also at the same facility, and also on Monday. She would be accompanying us on these visits and give us a tour of the hospital's cancer clinic, surgical center, imaging and nuclear medicine departments, while personally introducing us to doctors, nurses, and staff, who would be providing our care.

I knew I needed to provide unwavering support for Leslie as she went through this process, but I was way outside of my comfort zone in dealing with hospitals and doctors. I was scared to death and was unsuccessfully trying not to show it. At a minimum I needed to make sure Leslie was not worrying about me. With Kristi at our side, I at least had a chance of doing that much. Before we departed that evening with appointments and plan in hand, Kristi's husband Bob gave Leslie a bear hug and kiss and said, "Don't worry; we're going to take care of you."

I could see her breath flutter as he held her in his arms. His timing was perfect. It was one of the best things anyone has ever done for me. It is an image that will always be in my memory.

When we got home that night, I looked at Monday's appointments like they were baseball cards, searching online to find pictures and statistics. Our oncologist studied at Harvard Medical School and trained at the Dana-Farber Cancer Institute in Boston. I knew about that place! Its main fundraising arm is "The Jimmy Fund," the charity that partnered with the Boston Red Sox for the last fifty-plus years. During my first trip to Fenway Park the PA announcer explained the purpose of the fund, to fight childhood cancer, as donation cans were passed among the patrons. The second baseman on that 1967 World Series team, Mike Andrews, was the chairman of The Jimmy Fund for more than 25 years. I felt better already.

Our surgeon was a Midwesterner, coming from Ann Arbor, Michigan, and the University of Michigan Medical Center. Leslie would eventually develop such a strong bond with her that they exchanged text messages regarding the outcomes of surgeries and tests, shortening the agonizing waiting periods. It is in times like these that you can question any faith you have, but with me it was more of a realization that you had little control over life. The reoccurring connections to Michigan, New England and the Red Sox might be just coincidence or maybe something more.

Over the next weeks and months, Kristi was there with us, taking time from work as Leslie went through various rounds of procedures and surgeries. She also spent time with me in waiting rooms, keeping me calm. We learned a whole new language that included terms like sentinel node and positive margins. I did a pretty good job supporting Leslie throughout, but struggled at times when not in her presence. Kristi saw all of it and never wavered. As we rearranged life around this new reality, we decided to just tell people the truth as to why our plans changed. The response we got from friends was overwhelming. People kept track of Leslie's progress via email exchanges and phone calls with me. They marked their calendars with her key surgery dates and delivered meals and cheerful encouragement, often doing things directed specifically for me. People are generally busy and have family activities and obligations, but we felt we were temporarily part of a very large family. With all that support came the news we needed; Leslie would be making a full recovery.

While Leslie was recuperating from her final surgery, our friend, Jennifer, stopped by for a welcome visit on the back porch in Raleigh. I mentioned that I was planning a summer vacation as soon as Leslie was feeling up to it. Since moving from suburban Detroit, I had returned to see friends and play golf in Northern Michigan every year. I told Jennifer we were thinking of staying in Traverse City, Michigan, to explore the surrounding area, knowing that meant little to most folks in North Carolina who are unfamiliar with the Midwest.

Jennifer's face lit up: "Are you kidding? I grew up spending every summer at our family's cottage on Lake Leelanau!"

Jennifer went on to describe her memories and favorite activities that would make our trip special. I could see the anticipation grow in Leslie. I was happy she was looking forward to it and not completely focused on her short-term recovery. Jennifer had raised our spirits that day and assured us we would love our upcoming excursion in Northern Michigan. As she left she mentioned that her childhood friends from Lake Leelanau had settled in Traverse City. They were brothers, one an architect and the other an attorney.

That July we arrived at Cherry Capital Airport and immediately felt an attitude of genuine friendliness that pervaded our experience throughout the week. From the people at the lodge we stayed at, to the servers and patrons at restaurants in town, and almost everyone we met at local wineries and beaches, all seemed glad we were there. Leslie especially enjoyed the natural beauty of the area. The landscapes, plants and flowers, barns and farm stands, all reminded her of growing up in Central New York State.

Rick and his wife were on their way to Michigan's Upper Peninsula for a kayaking trip in the Channel Islands and had planned a stopover in Traverse City to coincide with our visit. They invited us to meet them for dinner at a restaurant on the Old Mission Peninsula. We decided to spend the afternoon prior to dinner exploring the peninsula, visiting some wineries and taking a look around. We were taken aback by the stunning vistas as we climbed the hills on the center road. I especially liked how it transitioned almost instantly to rural scenery.

Orchards and vineyards dotted with hillside barns, adorned with barn quilts, were all only a few miles out of town. We visited the winery where Rick was staying at their bed and breakfast perched on a hilltop with spectacular three hundred and sixty degree views. This confirmed our first impression of the beauty of the peninsula.

As we drove around Old Mission, I began to daydream about what it would be like to live there. I stopped at a couple of real estate signs with flyers for homes or lots for sale, confirming my intuition that it was probably beyond our means to own a place with lakefront or grand views. We passed one more real estate sign on the road along the bluffs of the East Bay. I grabbed a flyer and much to my surprise, the listed lake view home was more moderately priced than we expected. We set up an appointment, noting the work that would be required to update it, when we stepped onto the deck. We stopped in our tracks, forgetting our mental lists, caught up in the magnificent long-range bay views. The agent mentioned the adjacent lot was also for sale and we eagerly walked the bluff line lot discovering similar views. The lot was rugged and steep, and we were not sure how a home might sit on it. The price, reflecting the challenge of the lot, was attractive, which kept our dreaming alive. We were still holding on to our Cape cottage nest egg. Maybe this would be a place to put it to use?

Back at the lodge, we reflected on the day and the blend of excitement and angst that came with the bluff lot on the Old Mission Peninsula. If only we could know if it was suitable and buildable. We talked about our prior experience owning the cottage on Cape Cod, more landlords and handymen than residents, and our pledge to not repeat that experience. Years earlier, I had made a list of features and/or elements that we would change or add if we ever bought or built again.

Maybe it was affected by our recent health scare, but on our Michigan visit we made a decision to follow our instincts. We decided to use a day of our vacation to map out our dream house plan. I would try to recreate my sketches and lists while Leslie would email Jennifer back home and ask for the names of her childhood friends. Since we had not encountered an unfriendly face, maybe they could point us to folks that could help us evaluate our Old Mission ideas.

Cautiously, we knocked on the office door of architecture practice and asked if John, Jennifer's friend was in. Luckily he was, and we passed along greetings from Jennifer and asked for some advice on our real estate challenge. John warmly invited us in for a chat. We discovered that John worked exclusively in commercial architecture with many notable projects such as schools and harbor front developments. We were hopeful that John would direct us to a residential architect, or contractor who would be able to evaluate the Old Mission lot for suitability. As John asked more questions, I reached for my crude sketches and explained our goals and our inspiration drawn from the hillside barns on both the Leelanau and Old Mission peninsulas. To our great surprise, John said it sounded like a fun side project, and that the lot in question was not far from his home. He could take a look at it after work that evening! We had an immediate rapport with John and as we left we felt more than fortunate to have him involved in any capacity.

We made arrangements for other preliminary steps and the eventual purchase of the lot. We returned to vacationing with a trip to Sleeping Bear National Park. Sitting on the dunes looking out over the expanse of Lake Michigan, I smiled and thought about my first visit to the bluffs on the Atlantic in Cape Cod's National Seashore. I felt the same sense of calm and contentment here that I had as a child, college student, and vacationer looking down at the old life saving station at Coast Guard Beach. With time came perspective, and I came to the conclusion that I was very fortunate person. I just might be able to have that summer break by the shore I longed for every winter, not in Cape Cod, but on Lake Michigan.

There is nothing like a jarring encounter with illness to make you realize all your long-range plans don't add up to much on paper. I was a planner by trade. I was a project manager with large technology companies, I spent some time as a financial planner, and as general contractor on a house I flipped in Raleigh. I needed to change my focus from what could be achieved by age 65, to what would make memories now. Leslie had little apprehension when I suggested we start the building project immediately. We spoke with our architect John about general design schedules and costs and made plans for a Christmastime visit and meeting at his office.

We brought snapshots of barns from both of the peninsulas, my revised yet crude drawings, and a list of design elements. John was great in not dwelling on the obvious shortcomings of my work. Hallways too narrow, doors that won't open, etc. He was happy to stay within our size and cost constraints and embraced our notion of a slope-side barn with a stone clad foundation that would blend into the peninsula landscape.

We returned to Traverse City early in the summer and interviewed several local builders recommended by John. Our last interview was with 45th Parallel Construction Management and their two principles, Steve and Brad. Their approach meant subcontractors would be invited to bid on parts on the project based on prior work they had done for 45th Parallel and other projects with Steve and Brad. This approach would allow us to specify the custom work we wanted, along with some of the basic finishes, and have *only* that included in the competitive bidding process.

Steve from 45th Parallel reminded me of a smooth fielding shortstop on your softball team. You were always confident when the ball was hit to him. Our project team was coming together like my beloved Red Sox, who had suddenly found the right combination of players, attitude, and good fortune, to win two World Series in a four-year span. I felt Steve was going to get the right mix of players on our team. While we didn't agree on every task in the project, I always trusted his opinion. I think he was aware of this and seemed to share his reasoning in how he approached and managed the work. After reviewing the bids for the site work (clearing, grading, septic, well) and walking the lot one more time, ground was broken late in the fall.

We continued our tradition of Christmas in Traverse City. We arrived from North Carolina and climbed the hill to our lot on a snowy December afternoon, just in time to see the main beam arrive, followed shortly by the crane that would set it in place. We met many of the craftsmen working on the house.

Our last progress visit was on May 1st. As we made our way from the airport out to the peninsula site we found a sea of white. This time it wasn't snow, but field after field of white cherry blossoms. It was a scene that only Robert Frost could describe. The project was now moving to the interior finish stage. We could begin to see the fruits of John's design. The sight lines to the lake, the scoring of the concrete floor to create a finished look, and Leslie's outdoor shower design, were all integrated into a cohesive-feeling lake house that we began to refer to as the "skybarn."

Our first summer was hectic with finish work being completed on the decking, landscape and the driveway along with moving in and assembling the furniture. By late summer Leslie was able to organize a wrap party. We invited anyone who contributed to the project along with neighbors who witnessed both the progress and the disturbance associated with the construction. A bakery in town created a skybarn themed cake. We especially enjoyed some of the tradesmen showing off their work to their spouses who rarely see their husbands' work. It was a nice touch by Leslie and uncommon for a modest project like ours.

We now had a second home in every nature of the word and we continue to spend our summers and holidays in the skybarn. Tucked behind an interior sliding barn door, is the small office just as I had imagined it, the spot to write that book I wanted to, about growing up in Rhode Island.

Out on the deck looking at the lake, I twist off the cap off my second beer. I begin a mental game of trying to characterize the things, people, incidents, that stoked the flame of my Maditude over all these years. What was I really mad about? I was mad about being turned out into the world without getting any sense of confidence from Ed and Alice. Karen and I needed some idea that we were on equal footing with the rest of the world, regardless of the circumstances. The rest of the world is quick to tear you down and point out any shortcomings; you need the weapon of self-belief to combat it. Karen had struggled with this first and it had driven her to work harder and choose a vocation where she helped others and was appreciated for it. I reacted differently, overcompensating with an ultra competitive streak. Any chance to measure myself against others, took on an often-misplaced importance. I needed to be the one with the right answer, to win the game, get the girl, or win the praise of others. When things didn't go my way, I got mad. More importantly, when people didn't believe or wouldn't give me the chance to have the right answer, or win the game, I got Maditude. Inside this mostly negative quality there was a hidden positive attribute; a stubborn determination to achieve.

In hindsight, I choose to dwell on this positive aspect. That missing confidence was acquired through the years of striving to achieve some life goals. It was something I wanted from Ed and Alice, but I may have been asking for something they didn't have to give. I was trying to find it in my interactions with others, but discovered it's rarely conveyed. My Aunt Mae stood up and proclaimed that confidence in me at a crucial point. I need to try to do the same when interacting with nieces, nephews, and other young people.

The coincidence of our Raleigh friend Jennifer having Traverse City connections seemed more like fate to us. Her childhood friends assisted in turning the skybarn into reality. Jennifer continued to help us achieve some of our lifelong goals in another way. Jennifer is the executive director of a large community foundation in North Carolina. With her help, I served on the scholarship committee for one of the funds at the foundation that awards money for college to students who have overcome some adversity. I got great pleasure out of reading the essays and recommendations from the candidate pool. As I scored the applications, I found a candidate I thought most deserving, who eventually received the scholarship. I was speaking with the fund manager at the foundation and lamented about the scholarship only being a few thousand dollars, against the high cost of a college education. She said our scholarship winner also received something else.

"They get the confidence that we believe in them."

"Of course," I replied.

Leslie and I have set up our own fund at the foundation. It has a similar objective, to provide some of that confidence and funds for education to young people entering college, who might not be receiving it from traditional sources. It's called the Aunt Mae fund.

# Authors Note:

**Aunt Mae** lived out her years in my grandmother's house on Mauran Avenue. While she was housebound in her final years, she did come to our in-town wedding party and meet Leslie. Leslie and I had many visits with her at the house that we all cherished.

**Stephen** attended the University of Rhode Island and became a successful Information Technology professional. He continues to reside in Southern New England with his wife and children.

**Alice** lives independently in Riverside and is spending her golden years more positive and socially active. This includes a steady beau.

**Karen** continues to provide and manage speech therapy services in Southern New England where she lives with her family.

**E.T.** still resides in our childhood neighborhood with occasional excursions to act as the best man in our wedding or to visit us in North Carolina.

**Greg** resides with his wife and family in Southern New England. His father **Pete** moved to Florida to finish his career and retire in close proximity to many golf courses.

**Rockwell King** was still entertaining during summers at the Sand Bar as late as 2006. If you search YouTube you will find a video from that timeframe that shows Mike still working behind the bar and **Mary** at the front door.

**Rick** is still managing and mentoring people in the Information Technology industry. He remains a close personal friend.

**Leslie** and I are in our 22nd year of marriage and reside in Raleigh, North Carolina, and Traverse City, Michigan. I am determined to make this thing work despite all of the annoying habits of hers that I describe in the book.

# Acknowledgements

This book would not be possible without the constant support and belief of my wife Leslie. I'd also like to thank Mardi for her feedback and encouragement, Alice O. for her guidance, support, and skill editing the book, Jan for her design work, Janice for her feedback, and Bob for his technical assistance. I'd like to thank all of my friends and family who continue to listen to my ideas with patience and generosity.

DISCARD

Peninsula Community Library
2699 Island View Rd
Traverse City, MI 49686

JUL 2 4 2014
OCT DISCARD

Peninsula Community Library

4444045561333

Made in the USA
Charleston, SC
30 May 2014